"*Quick Calm* is a practical, accessible guide to help us leave the well-worn paths of stress and anxiety and navigate toward greater peace. This book reads like a wise friend speaking to you—and not just any friend, but one who's a brilliant neuropsychologist. *Quick Calm* is exactly the book we need right now. This very minute."

> **—Maggie Smith**, best-selling author of *Good Bones* and
> *Keep Moving*

"Jennifer Wolkin is a competent and kind guide who will accompany you on a journey to integrate mindfulness into your everyday life. She combines practicality and originality, offering both education and unique exercises designed to cultivate a consistent practice. *Quick Calm* is a resource you will return to again and again to help you live with less stress and more purpose."

> **—Alexandra H. Solomon, PhD**, clinical assistant professor at
> Northwestern University, licensed clinical psychologist, TEDx
> speaker, and author of *Loving Bravely* and *Taking Sexy Back*

"*Quick Calm* is a wonderful book for your meditation tool kit. With meditation 'how-tos' and thirty mindfulness exercises, it provides a dive into the present moment anywhere."

> **—Sharon Salzberg**, author of *Real Change*

"This delightful book will help you infuse all parts of living with a wakeful, open heart."

> **—Tara Brach**, author of *Radical Acceptance* and
> *Radical Compassion*

"Jennifer Wolkin has taken the guesswork and excuses out of getting in touch with your inner self and staying there. She has broken down the art of mindfulness in practical, easy-to-use ways that, if consistently incorporated, will enhance your everyday living for a lifetime. Everyone should have a marked-up, tattered copy of this book by their bedside. It's not a book; it's a survival guide."

—**Spirit, PhD, LPC, NCC**, national board-certified and
    licensed therapist, owner of T2S Enterprises, media personality,
    and mental health expert

"I would say that this book is a 'must-have-by-your-bedside' book anyway, but the fact that it's arrived during a global pandemic feels all the more fitting. Buy it for you and buy a copy for friends. Full of wisdom and grace, it's like an exhale when you've only been inhaling."

—**Jennifer Pastiloff**, author of *On Being Human*

"*Quick Calm* is an excellent resource that empowers us to approach our lives with more compassion and loving-kindness. The easy-to-follow steps are informative and nourishing. From seated meditation to mindfulness with everyday life tasks, this book enhances the journey to self-awareness and balance."

—**Thema Bryant-Davis, PhD**, licensed psychologist,
    ordained minister, author, and host of *The Homecoming Podcast*
    with Dr. Thema

"In *Quick Calm* by Jennifer Wolkin, the reader is gifted with practical tools to cultivate a mindfulness practice. She outlines the importance of meditation and gives you the power to cultivate a more peaceful, less stressful life. I highly recommend this to people who are seeking to have deeper awareness and more fulfillment."

—**Nicole LePera, PhD**, holistic psychologist, and
    author of *How to Do the Work*

Quick Calm

Easy Meditations to Short-Circuit Stress Using Mindfulness & Neuroscience

JENNIFER R. WOLKIN, PhD

New Harbinger Publications, Inc.

Publisher's Note

This publication is designed to provide accurate and authoritative information in regard to the subject matter covered. It is sold with the understanding that the publisher is not engaged in rendering psychological, financial, legal, or other professional services. If expert assistance or counseling is needed, the services of a competent professional should be sought.

NEW HARBINGER PUBLICATIONS is a registered trademark of New Harbinger Publications, Inc.

Distributed in Canada by Raincoast Books

Library of Congress Cataloging-in-Publication Data

Names: Wolkin, Jennifer R., author.
Title: Quick calm : easy neuroscience-based mindfulness meditations to short-circuit stress / Jennifer R. Wolkin, PhD.
Description: Oakland, CA : New Harbinger Publications, [2021] | Includes bibliographical references.
Identifiers: LCCN 2020042656 (print) | LCCN 2020042657 (ebook) | ISBN 9781684036080 (trade paperback) | ISBN 9781684036097 (pdf) | ISBN 9781684036103 (epub)
Subjects: LCSH: Mindfulness (Psychology) | Stress (Psychology) | Stress management.
Classification: LCC BF637.M56 W656 2021 (print) | LCC BF637.M56 (ebook) | DDC 158.1/3--dc23
LC record available at https://lccn.loc.gov/2020042656
LC ebook record available at https://lccn.loc.gov/2020042657

Printed in the United States of America

23   22   21

10   9   8   7   6   5   4   3   2

To Jacob, Alex, and Joey:

My hearts, I love you to the quasars and back.

Contents

Part 4: Mindful Living

Foreword

I remember nothing from any of the nights I won my Olympic Gold medals.

I only remember smoothing my Team USA uniform a bit before walking toward the spot where I would begin my run on the long jump runway. I remember taking a deep centering breath before rocking forward to take my first step.

My memories of each of those events have been crafted by YouTube videos, social media, and retellings from friends and family, fans and followers that witnessed them. This isn't unusual, there's a place that elite athletes have the ability to go to—or I should say...can withdraw to—that puts them fully in the present moment. With nothing to look back on, or look forward to—it's a space where all there is, is to be and do. It's often referred to as "the zone," and I navigate this space with ease; or at least I had.

But in the pursuit of my nine medals (so far), life happened to me, as it happens to us all, and I began to live in a new space—one where I ruminated on the past and fretted over the future.

I became exhausted by the constant suffering that living everywhere but in the "here and now" created in me. So I did the only thing I could think of to do, I ran away to Italy!

I met Dr. Jen in 2019 in an aging Tuscan villa that sat alone in lavender-laced Italian countryside. We were gathered there for a yoga retreat led by a mutual friend. We did not know each other but because we were seated close to each other we were paired together on the first activity asked of our group. We were meant to turn to our partner and look into their eyes, without speaking, until the timer went off. Turning to face each other, we clasped hands and stared into each other's eyes. I took in her face, open and trusting, warm and calm.

Maybe it was five minutes, maybe it was forever. But I remember wondering if she could see me. An interesting thought to have while staring at someone staring back at you. I saw in her beautiful eyes not just the myriad of colors it takes to make her particular shade of brown but a willingness—no…an invitation—to be here…now. An open invitation to sit with her, to breathe deeply with her, to be here, together, now.

I nodded slightly as if to say, "I accept," and, as if receiving that telepathic message, she squeezed my hand a little more tightly, a small smile flitting across her lips while her face became blurred by my eyes filling with tears. It was perhaps the first time since my marriage (and my inevitable divorce) that I had been truly present outside of a track and field competition, and yet the sensation was familiar. It was a "zone" of sorts. Only this time it was not a track coach that guided me to the finish line, but this woman, my new soul sister Jen, who was literally holding my hands and would be absolutely integral in my journey to find my way home.

As the retreat went on I continued to seek Jen out, to settle in on the couch cushion nearby to chat for five minutes, or unroll my yoga mat across the floor near hers. Day after day she reminded me of the importance of being gentle with myself, to give myself credit for showing up, to pat myself on the back for the accomplishments of the past but to not stay there; rather to simply allow the ghosts of gold medals past to propel me forward to bigger and better goals I may have for myself.

I know I am not alone when I say I can be my harshest critic, both on and off the track. We all need a person like Jen reminding us of the importance of being gentle with ourselves, and to simply begin again when we "mess it up" rather than assigning blame and judgment and guilt.

If comparison is an act of violence to oneself, then the constant comparing of who I am currently to the person I was over four years ago at the last Olympic Games is the ultimate act of self-harm. "Gentle, gentle, gentle," she reminds me. "Breathe, beauty," she says, either through text or on our coveted video calls.

Jen is the coach we need. The type that coaxes greatness from a person with compassion. With open arms and open doors, and a knowledge backed by so many scientific facts that even when I don't believe in myself and my abilities, I believe in her and her brain, and it's enough to pull me through!

As I write this, step by step, we continue to walk together through one of the most unpredictable years in all our lives. Call after call, even while navigating her own pains and frustrations, Jen holds space for me, returning my awareness to the present, to the breath, to all the things that are true, and to my ability to drop in and drag greatness from myself in huge moments.

However, one of the most important things I have picked up from Jen, whether directly through her work or indirectly through our friendship, is that the ability to drop into "the zone" no longer needs to be reserved for huge moments like the Olympic finals. This calm can be cultivated in the day-to-day, in the mundane. I can be present and mindful upon waking, while I'm driving or cleaning, or training and competing.

And my god the benefits! To possess the ability to hold the power of (quite literally) changing our minds is a gift we no longer need to squander. I practice daily to prepare my physical body; I've learned we all have the ability to access this mindfulness practice every day as well. Yet, unlike my athletic training, it doesn't require hours upon hours each day, but just five minutes. And just as I wasn't born an elite athlete and didn't become an Olympic champion overnight—it's the result of committed effort over a really long period of time—mindfulness is a practice that requires sustained effort. Moments at a time, day after day. And just as I did when I stood atop the podium singing the national anthem with a gold medal draped about my neck, you will get to a "mountaintop" or podium moment in your life and reflect on how far you've come, and how it was not a miracle but the result of you embracing your powerful daily practice, day after day after day.

All any of us has to do is start and, when we falter, start again. And if you're feeling like you don't know where to start, let me remind you of this most important thing: you are here, and Dr. Jen is here guiding you to and through how to make your already powerful mind your biggest ally.

—Tianna Bartoletta

PART 1

Prepractice

CHAPTER 1

Just Give Yourself Five!

Have you ever noticed your mind racing with excessive worry and thoughts of uncertainty? Do you have a deep overwhelm that your to-do list will never get done? Are life's external stressors; work deadlines, family responsibilities, financial issues, health concerns, and/or relationship commitments impacting your health and well-being? Are your internal negative thoughts creating anxiety by whispering that joy, love, and contentment are not yours to own? Maybe you have felt the burden of self-doubt that you're not enough, that you don't matter, and that accomplishing a goal is out of reach. Does any of this ring true?

It definitely did for me when I was struggling with what was eventually diagnosed as endometriosis. Years of stress and pain left me feeling invalidated and helpless. Negative self-talk seeped in, making it difficult to concentrate on my personal life, my career, and my aspirations. I found myself disconnecting from my relationships, and avoiding even simple daily tasks. I was anxious and overwhelmed.

That's when, in searching for something to help my mind and body settle, I discovered mindfulness. In turning to this practice, I could not have predicted the positive long-term impact it would have on my overall well-being. Mindfulness practice, as you will see, is more than "just a breathing exercise," but the breath was my starting point. As I cultivated my ability to focus on my breath, I became more present to the moment as it was actually unfolding. Just five minutes a day of mindfulness practice allowed me to purposefully take a pause, and tune into the present moment with less judgment and more self-compassion.

Stress can wreak havoc on our overall well-being and ability to function, and I wrote this book as a tool to help you short-circuit stress. So, are you ready to join me? All I will ask is for you to set aside five minutes of your time each day. Carving out bits of time, as I do, each and every day, cues the brain to authentic and lasting healing. I am looking forward to embarking on this journey together.

Finding Five Minutes

I understand that time is one of the most valuable resources you have. In a world where doing more, and doing more faster is celebrated, even dedicating five minutes for mindfulness practice might sound unrealistic, or perhaps a bit daunting. Looking at your jam-packed daily schedule of personal and professional commitments can make the thought of taking time out of your day seem impossible.

The thing about five minutes is, it's more than zero minutes. Mindfulness—even in small doses—adds up, especially when it's practiced every day.

But does five minutes a day really help? Absolutely. Our brain thrives on repetition. It's similar to lifting weights. Hoisting five- to ten-pound weights for five minutes a day, every day, can change your physique and make you stronger. The changes won't happen overnight, but in time, the results will become noticeable because our muscles, like our brain, respond to consistency. In fact, practicing five minutes a day has a bigger payoff for your well-being over the long term than practice for one hour once a week.

Of course, it's hard to measure the brain's progress because you can't actually see your neural circuitry forming new healthy connections in the mirror, in the same way you can see your muscles strengthening. Yet, over time, you will certainly feel it.

Muscles and mirrors aside, my commitment to you is to guide you through five-minute mindfulness practices throughout this book. Sometimes we'll build these five minutes into activities you are already engaging in anyway (like walking to work or drinking coffee.) Other times, we'll take five minutes to intentionally slow down to notice the breath or scan the body. Either way, we will be doing this together. I will not stop advocating for you to "try on" being gentler with yourself, to allow yourself time to reset and return to the busyness of everyday life after a restorative pause, in the form of five minutes.

How to Use This Book

This book is designed to be engaged with over and over again and will be most effective when used as a guide that sits on a night table or coffee table rather than on your bookshelf. This guide will lay out for you what "mindfulness" means, what mindfulness practice entails, and how mindfulness will help to rewire your brain for less stress and anxiety, increased calm and less reactivity, decreased chronic pain, and an overall healthier you. I will help you set up a practice and navigate some of the challenges to practicing, and I will offer up bite-sized practices of all kinds.

The next two chapters will explain more about what mindfulness is and introduce the how-tos of practicing. The thirty mindfulness exercises that follow are organized into formal, informal, and mindful living practices. In the how-tos of practicing in chapter 3, I will talk about how to get the most out of doing these different types of practice.

You'll also find some helpful materials available for download at the website for this book: http://www.newharbinger.com/46080. (See the very back of this book for more details.)

Who Is This Book For?

This book is for you! It is for anyone who wants to nurture greater well-being. Our human capacity for well-being is intrinsic, and this book helps you leverage it. Likely, you are drawn to this book because you may want to:

- Add to a well-being toolkit or start building one to navigate intrinsic life stressors, the ups, the downs, the all-arounds

- Learn to de-stress in the face of a specific stressor, such as work or school deadlines

- Learn ways to cope with chronic pain

- Reduce chronic stress

- Reduce anxiety that might be interfering with multiple areas of functioning

- Increase your ability to focus on specific tasks

- Increase your ability to stay present in relationships and improve them

- Increase self-compassion

- Cultivate a self-care practice

- Live life less on autopilot and with more purpose, on purpose

Any or all of these reasons may be motivating you to seek greater well-being through mindfulness.

Self-Care, You Dare!

Many of us tell or have heard the false story that "Self-care is selfish." We may have the unhelpful perception that either one cares for oneself or one is selfish! But through continued practice, you, like me, will see the amazing pay-it-forward effect of mindfulness, specifically, and self-care more generally. When we actually do the work of taking the time to tune ourselves, as if we were a precious instrument within a robust orchestra, everyone benefits. I certainly wouldn't want to play a cello that was out of tune. Believe me, I've tried!

The moral of this metaphor is that self-care actually benefits everyone around us. When we take the time to tune ourselves, to listen to our bodies and minds when they need to rest, refuel, and regroup, we have more capacity to be there for others in our lives. We have room and reserves to show up for those who need us. I challenge you to reframe your own story of what self-care is or isn't, to see for yourself how taking care of yourself creates dividends for those you show up for.

Engaging in mindfulness practice isn't about fixing anything, because we are not broken! It's about learning to navigate the ebbs and flows of life, to learn to acknowledge barriers that try to keep us from feeling well and to notice the open and expansive fields of possibility for experiencing joy.

(Important note: If you are unable to get out of bed in the morning, or if your anxiety is so overwhelming that you are not able to leave your house, please reach out to a mental health professional. The same goes if you are suffering from the impact of a traumatic experience. Reaching out to a psychologist while engaging in mindfulness meditation means that you are allowing yourself the room to take care of yourself on a deeper level, to grow healthy tissue around some old scars, to shed the shame we sometimes associate with feeling emotional or physical pain.)

I'm glad we are going to be together for five minutes each day. This is a big step, and I'm here with you. Next, I'm going to delve into what mindfulness truly means so that you have a solid sense of what you are practicing, and why. I find that this information often helps my brain prepare to show up!

CHAPTER 2

What Is Mindfulness, and Why Practice?

Mindfulness meditation is an actual practice (an action) used to cultivate more *mindfulness* (a state of being). So, in the purest sense of the term, "mindfulness meditation" is situated under the bigger umbrella of "meditation," which can be any technique or practice used to gain mental clarity. For the purposes of this book, I refer to "mindfulness meditation" as "mindfulness practice."

From a historical perspective, mindfulness practice is thousands of years old. While many religions and cultures have taught the tenets of mindfulness, Buddhism holds mindfulness at its core probably more than any other tradition. According to ancient Buddhist philosophy, mindfulness was practiced with the goal of the cessation of personal suffering.[1]

In more recent times, mindfulness has been applied as a secular adjunctive technique to Western psychological interventions. This began in the 1970s with Jon Kabat-Zinn's use of mindfulness to help people with chronic pain relate to their suffering in an alternative way. Since then, mindfulness has been adapted to treat a variety of psychological conditions and assist in overall stress reduction. Kabat-Zinn has defined mindfulness as a state of greater awareness cultivated by paying attention *on purpose, in the present moment,* and *nonjudgmentally.*[2]

Paying Attention on Purpose

When we don't hone our focus, on purpose, we tend to operate on autopilot. Do you know that feeling of being disconnected from yourself, when you're on autopilot? This is when we get lost in *doing,* and we find ourselves striving and struggling to get stuff done instead of being in the present and really appreciating the moments of our lives. We may even do things when we're on autopilot that are harmful to ourselves or others. In contrast, when we are attentive on purpose, we start to live more consciously. We're more awake and more fully ourselves, and we notice the beauty of life.

Engaging in the Present Moment

Mindfulness is also about engaging in the present moment, as the human mind habitually wanders away from it. When we are not in the here and now, we may dwell in the past, grasping and replaying it, or project into the future, trying to anticipate the unknown (and often catastrophizing). This doesn't mean we can't fondly remember something or plan for our futures, but when we obsess about the past or about the future in an effort to manipulate what we can't control, we place ourselves at greater risk for depression and anxiety.

For example, have you ever gone over and over a certain experience in your head and continued to ask yourself, *Why did I say this instead of that?* or even *Why did I let this happen in the first place?* It's natural to want to go back in your mind so that you can somehow correct what happened, yet it's hamster-wheel thinking, because as much as you want to go back to change something, the reality is that you can't.

Likewise, hanging out in the future is a way of trying to maintain perceived control over our lives, because the unknown is uncomfortable. The reality is, we really can't control the future, no matter how much we want to. There are things we can control, like how much we train for a race or when we go to sleep or what and how we eat. For the most part, though, beyond the little everyday lifestyle choices we can make, the future is out of our control.

When mindful, we hone our clarity and focus as we attend to every sensation as it unfolds, engaged in the present-moment experience. When we accept the present moment as it is, we let go of the tension caused by wanting things to have been or to be different.

Noticing Nonjudgmentally

When practicing mindfulness, we're not trying to control, suppress, or stop our thoughts. We don't want to push our thoughts away (it's not even possible to do so). Rather, mindfulness helps us pay attention to our experiences as they arise, without judging or evaluating them in any way. This is the essence of mindfulness. When we cultivate a state of clarity in which we suspend judgment, we become witnesses of our present-moment experience. Sure, there's temptation to judge that experience as good or bad. Yet, letting go of judgments helps us see things as they are rather than through the filters of patterned and conditioned modes of thinking. This way, we are less likely to mechanically play out old habitual ways of thinking and living.

So, in other words, mindfulness is, one, the state of consciously and deliberately noticing what we are attending to instead of remaining on autopilot and, two, doing so without attaching judgment. Boiled down, practicing mindfulness is a way to practice when and how we attend to the stimuli in our internal environments (thoughts, feelings, sensations) and external environments (interpersonal interactions, the physical world). Cultivating our attention allows us to stay present to each moment as it unfolds. Staying present, nonjudgmentally, allows us to let go of negative *rumination,* which is a passive dwelling upon negative thoughts and emotions[3]—a state nicknamed the *wandering mind.* In this way, mindfulness, the cultivation of attention on purpose, in the present moment, and without judgment, becomes a tool to stave off chronic stress, anxiety, and depression, or all of the above.

Of course, there is no way to keep our mind from wandering, and there is no such thing as completely clearing our minds. In fact, an important part of practicing mindfulness and creating a mindfulness state is to notice our wandering mind with compassion, loving-kindness, and nonjudgment. Then, we can practice using our attention to either bring our mind back to the present moment or continue following our wandering mind as a nonjudgmental witness.

The Stories We Tell

Each of us has a story we tell to make sense of ourselves in the world. Sometimes this story is told through filters we developed when we were very young and first trying to make sense of our external and internal worlds through the lenses of society and those around us. Sometimes we make unconscious agreements with ourselves that *This must be who I am*, and a story becomes a habit. Sometimes a story develops to protect us from trauma, and it works—until it doesn't. For example, you may create a story that separates you from your pain, which feels better in the moment—and many moments after that—but eventually that same story starts to create more pain as you evolve and realize that, when you shut down, your ability to see your true self is clouded and you have difficulty connecting with others.

But here is the most amazing thing about a story: it's just a story! Are there certain stories you know you are telling yourself that aren't true and that don't serve you? If so, all I am going to ask is that you hold them without judging them.

Of course, it's not always so easy to even know the story we are telling. That's where mindfulness practice can be of service. Mindfulness practice allows us to get in touch with this story. The story is often on autopilot, and it's not until we allow ourselves to notice our thought process, the feelings and sensations it elicits, that we become aware of it at all.

Much of the time, our stories are self-protective yet lead to suffering. When we catastrophize, our minds wander down a rabbit hole of negative *what-ifs?* While our brains are wired with a built-in protective mechanism, sometimes we overprotect. Our brains go from adaptive caring to a hypervigilance that leads to great suffering. In this space, we aren't trusting in the possibility of thriving.

Here's the empowering part of this: you can train your brain to understand that even in the context of future-oriented thinking, it is much more likely that things will be okay and, in fact, more than okay! That's where the work begins, and a journey of more adaptive, real, less-filtered, less-skewed storytelling can and will unfold.

If you pay attention with compassion, anything is possible. This includes even the rewriting of stories that once worked for you to protect yourself but now are perhaps blocking your way to a life lived on purpose.

Mindfulness and the Brain

World-renowned neuroscientist Richard Davidson proposes that we can actually train our brains to change—and that this change is measurable.[4] Davidson is referring to the concept of *neuroplasticity*, which is the brain's ability to create new neural connections and form new pathways based on our experiences and what we learn. This idea of a malleable brain wasn't always so popular. Not too long ago, most researchers thought that after a certain age (by early adulthood), the neural circuitry cards we've been dealt were the only ones we could play in our lives. In other words, researchers believed that adult brains were not capable of change.

These days, there is more evidence to the contrary: it turns out that the brain is in a constant state of change and is designed to adapt. So far, researchers have noted that the brain can change both structurally (its physical structure) and functionally (how one part of the brain talks to another part). What this means is that every new thing that we learn (including mindfulness practice) has the potential to reinvent our brain and therefore ourselves. We can change our current operating system and rewire our brain for increased well-being and decreased stress.

Mindfulness and Chronic Stress

Our brains are wired for survival, which, of course, is a type of well-being. After all, if our early ancestors hadn't survived dangers like the saber-toothed tiger, we wouldn't be talking about well-being right now! When we are on high alert, we go into what is called the *fight-or-flight* response, which is facilitated by part of our nervous system called the sympathetic nervous system. During fight-or-flight, the fear center of our brain (the amygdala) is more reactive, and our body releases hormones, including adrenaline and cortisol. These hormones increase our heart rate, dilate our pupils, increase glucose in the bloodstream, and curb bodily functions (like digestion) nonessential for taking immediate action to get away from the danger. Then, when the acute threat is gone, the brain and body ideally return to functioning as usual.

In the modern world, there may be no saber-toothed tigers, but as it turns out, we don't need to be physically threatened with life or death to go into a fight-or-flight response. We only need to be overworked, worried about finances, or juggling conflicting responsibilities and deadlines (the list goes on). It also turns out that we are often overworked, worried, and juggling responsibilities, so the fight-or-flight response is more often on than it is off, and our bodies are in high-alert mode for way longer than they were built to handle. This creates a state of chronic stress, the effects of which are systemic and associated with many health challenges, including hypertension, insomnia, and anxiety. Research indicates it can even negatively impact overall immune system functioning.[5]

Chronic stress is usually experienced when there is an inadequate match between our coping skills and environmental demands. *Coping skills* are the adaptive and effective ways we react to and interact with the demands of our environment. Mindfulness practice can be used to invoke the natural counterpoint to the fight-or-flight response, aptly called the *relaxation response*, also known as the rest-and-digest response.[6] During this response, our body no longer suspects it's in danger, and physiological relaxation occurs through the activation of the parasympathetic nervous system, which is a counterpoint to the sympathetic nervous system. Bloodstream cortisol and adrenaline levels decline, and heart rate, digestion, and other processes return to previous functioning.

Stress Reduction Vs. Stress Elimination

You might find yourself wanting to eliminate stress entirely, yet stress reduction is actually healthier than stress elimination. An appropriate stress response is a vital part of life. Aside from protecting us from very real environmental threats, we need a healthy amount of stress to motivate us to meet a deadline or study for a test or even learn something new. Our stress hormones, in moderation, help us to focus and create new memories, and improve mood. They are especially helpful when problems start to feel more like challenges, stimulating creative thinking and new brain connections. The ultimate goal, therefore, is to use adaptive levels of stress as a catalyst and reduce the stress that adds to suffering.

Research is still parsing out exactly how and why mindfulness practices reduce stress, but it is likely that the practice of cultivating attention on purpose, in the present moment, and nonjudgmentally helps reduce the stress elicited by past- or future-oriented thinking. Rumination often leads to stress and anxiety. Mindfulness practice can reduce this type of thinking (and the emotions and sensations it often leads to), which can only help us feel more relaxed and more in control of our thought processes.

Another avenue toward stress reduction through mindfulness is by stimulating the vagus nerve during formal practices like diaphragmatic breathing (see practice 1). The vagus nerve is one of the longest in the body, traveling all the way from brain stem to abdomen and snaking through many crucial organs like the heart and lungs. One of the most extraordinary facts about the vagus nerve is that it is instrumental in regulating heart rate and breath rate. When we lower our breathing rate, the vagus nerve notices (via connections from the heart and lungs) and, since we are breathing more slowly, tells the brain that there is no threat, it's okay to relax, and the parasympathetic nervous system has permission to take the reins.

Practice Makes Neuroplastic!

Recent studies have pointed to specific brain changes (neuroplasticity) that are the result of mindfulness practice. Many of these changes correspond to a less chronically stressed brain.[7]

Increased gray matter in the anterior cingulate cortex, the prefrontal cortex, and the hippocampus: The more robust the gray matter, the more efficient that region is. (Note: When referring to "gray matter," neuroscientists are referring to the part of the nerve cells, or neurons, that include the cell bodies, dendrites, and sometimes even nerve synapses.) The anterior cingulate cortex is a structure located behind the brain's frontal lobe. It has been associated with self-regulatory processes, including the ability to monitor attention conflicts and allow for more cognitive flexibility. The prefrontal cortex is primarily responsible for higher-order thinking and executive functioning, such as attentional control, planning, problem solving, and emotion regulation. The hippocampus is the part of the limbic system that governs learning and memory and is extraordinarily susceptible to stress and stress-related disorders like anxiety, depression, and post-traumatic stress disorder (PTSD).

Decreased amygdala size: Studies have shown that the brain-cell volume of the amygdala, the brain's fight-or-flight center and the seat of fearful and anxious emotions, decreases after mindfulness practice.

Strengthened connection between the amygdala and the prefrontal cortex: The functional connections between the amygdala and the prefrontal cortex strengthen with mindfulness practice. This allows the more logical captain of the human brain to steer with less reactivity and fear. When the prefrontal cortex is activated through regular mindfulness practice, higher-order responses to stress become the default, replacing go-to, fear-based responses.

Reduced activity in the medial prefrontal cortex (mPFC): The mPFC is sometimes referred to as the "me" center, because it's the part of the brain that is associated with the stories we tell about ourselves. Often, we are telling unhelpful negative stories, and our mind ruminates about mistakes we've made or how our future will turn out, for example. Though self-reflection can benefit us, consistent self-critical self-referential loops impact our well-being and can lead to depression and anxiety. Neuroimaging research shows decreased activity in this "me" center after mindfulness practice. Mindfulness practice can help us ungrasp from this wandering mind and, instead, learn to focus our attention away from thoughts of how our life "should be" and toward present-moment reality.

These are some of the evidence-based ways that practicing mindfulness can actually change the brain, leading to less stress and greater wellness. As I like to say, practice makes neuroplastic!

Mindfulness and Anxiety

The words "stress" and "anxiety" are often used interchangeably, but it's good to differentiate between the two. For the most part, *stress* is emotional or physical pressure experienced due to an external cue (a stressor), like a work deadline or an impending move, that resolves once said stressor is alleviated. *Anxiety* is sometimes conceptualized as our response to stress and is elicited by more internal cues, such as catastrophic thinking or general worry.

"People with anxiety have a problem dealing with distracting thoughts that have too much power," explains psychiatrist Elizabeth Hoge. "They can't distinguish between a problem-solving thought and a nagging worry that has no benefit."[8] Mindfulness meditation practice hones the ability to be more discerning. We can then take action to solve problems, if possible, or to notice worries without judgment and with more compassion.

One of Hoge's studies found that after participating in mindfulness-based stress reduction (MBSR), participants had a decrease in their generalized anxiety greater than the control group (those who didn't participate in mindfulness practice).[9] In another study, Hölzel, Hoge, and Greve found that subjects who participated in mindfulness practice were significantly less anxious than those who did not.[10] This study also linked positive changes on an anxiety scale to positive changes in brain regions associated with anxiety!

Mindfulness practice can help treat anxiety. It's a very beneficial tool that is often used with professional guidance and other therapeutic techniques. If you are experiencing anxiety that interferes with your usual activities or gets in the way of your daily functioning, please seek the help of a professional.

Mindfulness and Chronic Pain

Jon Kabat-Zinn was the first to study the connection between mindfulness meditation and pain.[11] In a 1985 study, ninety chronic-pain patients were trained in MBSR. Results indicated statistically significant reductions in measures of present-moment pain, negative body image, inhibition of activity by pain, mood disturbance, and psychological symptomatology, including anxiety and depression. Additionally, pain-related drug use was reduced. Since then, there have been many more studies with similar findings.

Pain is a complex phenomenon. When we first experience a sensation of pain, we begin to judge it as bad and as something we want to immediately eradicate. Then, we start to conspire ways to escape the pain, to find any solution we can come up with, all the while continuing to judge our pain as negative. The subjective judgment we add inflates the pain, making the experience of it far more noxious than the sensory experience alone.

Mindfulness meditation provides pain relief by cultivating the ability to parse the objective sensory dimension of pain and the more subjective judgment that we attach to the pain and that constructs the way we experience it. Mindfulness practice can be used to create more awareness of the sensation of pain itself, without the judgment or resistance that we often project upon it. When we impose a litany of negativity upon our pain, it only becomes worse, and potentially elicits other difficulties, including depression and anxiety. When we become more aware of what we are actually experiencing, without the overlay of judgment, the overall perception of pain decreases.

Even though focusing on the sensory experience of pain may sound counterproductive, it actually provides a pathway to pain relief that is different from the traditional pharmacologic interventions that aim to quell the sensation of pain immediately. Remember, what causes actual suffering is not the pain (though pain is, yes, painful) but the story we tell ourselves about it!

Mindfulness and Immune Function

The immune system is one of the most critical purveyors of our physical well-being. It is so precisely designed that it can distinguish between harmful unwanted pathogens and our own healthy cells and tissue. The immune system has even been referred to as our "floating brain" for its ability to communicate with the brain through chemical messages that float around inside our body. This means that if our immune system is weakened, perhaps as a result of chronic stress or other causes, our whole body system won't operate as usual. When our immune system struggles, it's like a welcome sign for infection and disease. Thankfully, there is increasing evidence that mindfulness practice boosts the immune system.

A recent and groundbreaking review looked at twenty randomized controlled trials examining the effects of mindfulness meditation on the immune system.[12] In reviewing the research, the authors found that mindfulness practice:

1. Reduced markers of inflammation, high levels of which are often correlated with decreased immune functioning and disease

2. Increased the number of CD-4 cells, the immune system's helper cells, which are involved in sending signals to other cells telling them to destroy infections

3. Increased telomerase activity; telomerase helps promote the stability of chromosomes and prevent their deterioration

In another study, people were injected with the flu vaccine and were either part of a group receiving mindfulness training or a control group. After eight weeks, the mindfulness group had greater levels of antibodies available to respond to, and prevent, potential illness.[13]

Mindfulness and Emotion Regulation

In many situations, we can choose either to react from a place of fear and perhaps anger or to respond more mindfully. Reacting is a reflexive, and sometimes impulsive, way to behave that often precludes thinking before doing something. To reiterate, many of our reactions come from a brain that is in survival mode. When we are in this state, it is some-times hard to regulate emotions without the input of a greater aware-ness of what a given situation requires. When we engage in fear-based behaviors, we start to ruminate and tell stories about ourselves that are less than helpful. But rather than just reacting in this way, we can take a more mindful approach in any given situation.

As psychiatrist and Holocaust survivor Viktor Frankl said, "Between stimulus and response there is a space. In that space is our power to choose our response. In our response lies our growth and our freedom." To respond in lieu of reacting, we need to proceed with more mindful awareness.

Whereas *reacting* is a reflexive, and sometimes impulsive, way to behave in a situation, *responding* is a more mindful approach that involves observation, reflection, and purposeful procession. Just one extra moment to pause, take a step back, regroup, and consider a healthier response can make a huge difference. It's becoming clearer to researchers that practicing mindfulness meditation can help us regulate our emotions and lash out at one another less often!

As mentioned earlier in this chapter, mindfulness meditation is associated with increased connection between the amygdala and the prefrontal cortex. This leads to greater integration of our emotions and intellect. How does this help? Here's an example: When your romantic partner or boss or even child says something that hurts, you may feel threatened. That activates the amygdala that readies you to attack back. But instead of impulsively trying to attack, mindfulness practice can help you respond, with compassion for the pain that both you and the other person are experiencing, by truly listening and then answering from a place that is less fear based.

Slowly, but steadily, you can work together with others to decrease your amygdala's activity! It's hard, but imagine if both people in a partnership practiced taking a few breaths before lashing out and attacking and instead responded with a calmer and less-defensive demeanor. They'd actually give one another the space to be heard and the opportunity to communicate without armor. When you are not in imminent danger, but you are still on that precipice at which your sympathetic nervous system is gearing up for a fight-or-flight reflexive reaction, you need to take a mindful moment before reacting. When your body is just about to unleash a cascade of increased stress hormones and your mind is roaring with resentment and anger, you can pause until you are ready to respond.

The great irony is that by stopping for just one moment, you are really moving. You are moving into your own self and out into the world with greater presence and a more mindful disposition. The more you practice mindful living, the richer your interactions and experiences, and the more you thrive. A quote from Mahatma Gandhi comes to mind here: "You can't change how people treat you or what they say about you. All you can do is change how you react to it." Mindfulness practice is, in part, becoming aware that you are only responsible for your own self: you can't change the way anyone else shows up in any situation ever, no matter how much you want to or how much you try. Mindfulness practice is also about taking responsibility for the way you show up in response to others.

Why Practicing Is So Important

If you ever have doubts about taking five minutes a day, every day, for mindfulness practice, return to this list. Review why doing this is so important:

1. Mindfulness practice will allow you to live with greater awareness, as you attend to life on purpose, and with less judgment —maybe even with more compassion!

2. Mindfulness practice can help reduce your level of suffering through greater awareness of the unhelpful stories you are telling about yourself and your experience of chronic pain.

3. Mindfulness practice provides you with the coping skills to recognize life's stressors and can help you reduce stress to levels that fuel you appropriately.

4. Mindfulness practice can help ease anxiety.

5. Mindfulness practice will benefit your immune system and support your overall mental, emotional, physical, and cognitive well-being.

6. Mindfulness practice will not eliminate life's pressures, but it can help you respond to them in a less-reactive, more adaptive, and healthy manner.

7. Mindfulness practice for five minutes a day every day reminds your brain that it has the capacity to wire for wellness.

Mindfulness practice will require a conscious effort and hard work, but it is a continuous journey! Feel free to reread this list before you practice or any time you want motivation to maintain your ongoing practice. You can even bookmark this page for your reference.

CHAPTER 3

The How-Tos of Practice

I want to dispel the notion that mindfulness meditation is all about breathing on a cushion somewhere in a quiet and isolated room. While breathing is a great mindfulness meditation to start with (and part 2 will start with a breathing practice), it's not the only way at all! I like to think of three categories of mindfulness practice to engage in for increased well-being. The exercises in this book are culled from these three.

Formal practice. Formal meditation, also known as "on the cushion," entails intentionally taking time out of your schedule and finding a specific physical space to embark on meditative practice. This time gives you an opportunity to bear witness to your mind and to understand and reflect upon habitual tendencies with a sense of kindness and curiosity rather than judgment. Practices 1 through 10 introduce formal meditation.

Informal practice. Practicing informally means you don't need to be sitting somewhere specific to stay nonjudgmentally present (paying attention) to every sensation as it unfolds. Informal mindfulness meditation means you can rest in mindful awareness at any time of day, no matter what you're doing: washing dishes, walking, taking a shower. There is a Zen saying that "when you drink, just drink, and when you walk, just walk." This sums up informal mindfulness practice. Practices 11 through 22 offer opportunities to engage in informal meditation.

Mindful living. You begin to live mindfully when your continued formal and informal mindful meditation practices positively impact your relationship with yourself and relationships with others. Mindfulness then becomes more than a practice. It is not so much a meditation as the by-product, so to speak. It's a way of life that encompasses, for example, values of gratitude, loving-kindness, and compassion. Practices 23 through 30 focus attention on mindful living.

Practice Guidance

All of the exercises in this book will benefit you. No practice is better or worse than another. What matters, however, is that you find an exercise that resonates with you and that helps you cultivate a continued practice. Give each exercise a chance, since sometimes it may take getting used to the meditation in order to benefit from it. Anything new can be uncomfortable at first. If, after a few times, you are noticing a strong resistance, and you aren't feeling any sense of increased well-being, then please move on. If you find a practice you particularly like, you can bookmark it and come back to it whenever you want.

Here are a few more practicing insights.

There's No Right or Wrong Way

If you find yourself practicing and notice the thought *I am doing this all wrong*, it's important to challenge that thought by reminding yourself that, literally, there is no wrong way to practice. There is just showing up. Some days your practice might feel different than it does on other days. Some days you might feel more distracted, less relaxed, and maybe even restless. Other days, you might feel less distracted, more relaxed, and maybe even more grounded. It's all okay! Also, practice makes practice, not perfect.

It's Never Too Late to Start Over

I want to let you in on the secret that changed my mindfulness practice and my overall sense of living a life on purpose: it is never too late to start over. I mean this deeply. The one thing I learned in graduate school and during postdoc, and beyond is that most things take many starts. The key is showing up and, as excruciating as it sometimes is, starting over again. The possibility to start again doesn't ever stop, and that is the absolute beauty of life. If you start a practice and then miss a day or two—or seven, or seventy, or even seven hundred—you can start again. Really. Watch the judgment of *I can't believe I couldn't make this last*, offer up compassion, and then begin again. It's a simple concept, but not easy.

In mindfulness practice, consistency and compassion for inconsistency are both key. Remember, the impact that mindfulness practice exerts on our brain is born from routine: a slow, steady, and consistent reckoning of our realities and the ability to take a step back, become more aware, more accepting, less judgmental, and less reactive. Just as playing the piano over and over again, over time, strengthens and supports brain networks involved with playing music, mindfulness over time can make the brain, and thus you, a more efficient regulator, with a penchant for pausing to respond to your world instead of mindlessly reacting. Oh, and there is no race. Only showing up. You are not competing with anyone, not even yourself.

So two essentials to keep in mind are consistency of practice and compassion for when you're not consistent and need to start again. That's the beauty of it all. You can change your brain to work more efficiently for you, and there is no end to the number of times you can try.

Your Mind Will Wander

During any of these practices, you might notice thoughts pulling you into the past or the future. Your mind might be pulled toward certain thoughts, feelings, physical sensations, fantasies, dreams, and even to-do lists. You might notice feelings coming up that seem all-encompassing. You might notice nagging sensations. Whatever comes up, it is absolutely okay. There is nothing wrong with you—in fact, there is everything human about you. Minds wander. See if you can offer up a gentle awareness to whatever comes up.

Whether you are practicing a formal sitting meditation, using the breath as your guide, or eating mindfully, see if you can notice a pull away from the object of meditation (such as the breath) without self-criticism and without self-judgment. Gently bring your attention right back. You might have to do this redirection many times. Know that this is natural and appropriate. The essence of mindfulness is non-judgmental awareness.

Seek Help if Needed

All of the practices in this book are designed to be done on your own. In certain cases, however, I would recommend that you do them under the guidance of a trained mental health professional. If you are currently experiencing the impact of trauma, such as PTSD, please proceed with caution. This doesn't mean you can't do these exercises. A lot of evidence supports mindfulness as a treatment approach for adults with PTSD, and burgeoning literature suggests mindfulness practice can result in positive neurological changes for PTSD sufferers.[14] There is, without a doubt, great potential for this treatment in decreasing potential suffering. However, mindfulness practice by nature requires us to sit with a lot of uncomfortable thoughts, sensations, and emotions that can be quite triggering to anyone whose brain mechanisms are trying to do the opposite, which is to avoid sitting with self-awareness. If you think you might be triggered, mindfulness as an integrative approach under professional supervision would be prudent, so notice where you are, and reach out for the appropriate guidance if you feel it's needed.

If you have experienced dissociation, psychosis—including hallucinations or delusions—severe depression, severe mania, or severe anxiety that makes functioning difficult, I also recommend reaching out for help before practicing mindfulness. If any of these practices become too overwhelming, and you notice any of the above symptoms, please stop practice and reach out to your doctor.

Practice Logistics

Where should you practice? For most of these exercises, I recommend a quiet space with as few interruptions as possible. Of course, life is life, and we can't control everything in our environment (like barking dogs or subway train rumbles), so just do the very best you can.

When should you practice? It doesn't matter, but the key is to make practicing a habit. You may decide to practice formal meditation in the mornings when you wake up, for example. You can introduce mindfulness into your daily life by tacking a mindfulness practice onto a *keystone habit*—that is, a habit that serves as a pillar on top of which other interlocking habits can develop.[15] Keystone habits can cause a positive ripple in our lives. For example, establishing a physical exercise habit often leads to the habit of drinking more water, the habit of taking healthy supplements, a diet that is more nutritious, and so on. Here are some common keystone habits: making your bed every morning, taking a coffee break during the day, wiping down the kitchen counters after dinner, and getting regular exercise. You can do any of these activities mindfully. Do you have a keystone habit to which you can you link your mindfulness practice?

How to Move Through These Practices

You may want to begin with the first practice in part 2 and continue sequentially, moving your way through the formal, informal, and mindful living practices, but you do not need to move through these practices in any particular order. That being said, I do recommend starting with the breathing practice, which comes first. Breathing is used in some iteration in many exercises, and in my opinion, it's the foundation of all practice. The breath is grounding. It is always within us and available to use as a compass and a guide. Give yourself permission to relax into your breath and use it as a point of reference, a force within you that can be called upon anytime and anywhere to help you relax.

There are many ways to use this book effectively. Initially, I envisioned you spending five minutes a day (at least) on each practice for a week, starting with practice 1 and then proceeding to the next week's practice, and so on. However, I want you to be able to choose what works best for you. Consider starting with the breath, and then you can experiment as you'd like. If one of the formal practices calls to you, feel free to practice it for two weeks (or more), and if another doesn't call to you, feel free to return to it at a later time or not at all. It's okay to feel uncomfortable. The practices aren't easy, and I want you to practice in a way that supports your needs. Another option is to sample the formal, informal, and mindful living practices, as you see fit, to get a feel for the different types of practice as you move along. Again, my only strong recommendation is that you begin with the breath. Oh, and that after your timer hits five minutes, you can always feel free to reset it for as long as you need!

Formal Practice

Before you begin each formal practice, read the directions all the way through at least once. The idea is to eventually do the practice without having to read (and with your eyes closed).

When you're ready, get comfortable in a relatively quiet space. If you are seated, keep your back straight, but not stiff. Let your hands rest at your thighs or clasp them gently over your heart or abdomen. When you're instructed to soften your gaze, simply let your eyes relax and try not to focus on anything in particular.

Remember that your mind will likely wander during practice, and that's completely natural! With nonjudgment and compassion, just notice where it has wandered, and then redirect your attention back to the task at hand. You might have to engage in this redirection of attention multiple times during one practice. That's okay. It's very common. The practice is not only about training your attention to the present moment but also about cultivating compassion when your attention wanders and redirecting it without judgment.

After every formal practice, take a few moments before returning to your regular activity. As you get up, do so very gently and with care. You might feel more relaxed than usual, and perhaps even drowsy.

Informal Practice

Informal mindfulness practice allows you the opportunity to engage in everyday tasks with more conscious and purposeful awareness. Again, informal practice is the art of integrating mindfulness meditation into anything you're doing in your everyday life. Any activity that comes to mind, you can mindfully practice—and as long as you pay attention on purpose in the present moment and without judgment, you are practicing! Whatever action you are doing in any given moment, informal mindfulness practice entails focusing on that action by breaking it down into its smaller parts.

Informal practice starts with the premise that many of us are on autopilot as we move through our daily lives. It's my hope that these informal practices will help you tune in to the menial tasks and wake up to the often overlooked moments in your life.

There's much more research studying formal meditation, but current literature suggests that informal practice can be as efficient as formal practice at adding to your well-being. For example, a team led by Barbara Fredrickson studied the impact of informal mindfulness practice (such as mindful eating and mindful toothbrushing) on socioemotional well-being.[16] Results indicated that informal mindfulness practice is linked to both positive emotions and social integration in a dose-response fashion. In other words, the more often participants practiced informal meditation on a given day, the more they experienced both positive emotions and increased feelings of social connection on that day.

Each informal practice will have its own brief setup, and each is designed to be done for five minutes. For some practices, it might feel more intuitive to extend the time beyond five minutes. One day, it might feel right to extend your practice. The next, five minutes may be ideal for you. Use your own judgment, and go at your own pace. Choose what's best for you on any given day.

Again, your mind may wander during these informal practices. Let your thoughts come and go without rushing to figure out what they mean. Try to concentrate on what's happening in the moment, without judging or trying to change anything. As with formal practice, you can simply notice the thoughts and feelings and direct your attention back to the given practice.

The informal practices will include some specific follow-up questions that are meant to deepen your experience if you are interested. One day you might want to engage in these questions, and on another you won't. Whatever you choose to do is okay. Find the balance between sitting with healthy discomfort and listening to when you need to rest.

Mindful Living

I like to call the third category of practice "the sixth minute," because what you practice strengthens, gains momentum, and in time grows beyond the five-minute practice window and into the space of mindful living. Formal and informal practice is like a snowball. It takes momentum to build, but the more you roll it, the bigger it gets, touching beyond five minutes a day. Mindful living is that sweet spot where you can potentially live more fully.

The beauty of mindfulness is that once you engage in formal practice and then incorporate informal practice into your everyday tasks, you begin to watch it become a way of life. You start to experience a shift in the lens through which you view experience in general. Mindful living is still about paying attention and doing so without judgment, yet it's on a more global scale. It's about standing in your self-worth, offering up compassion, self-care, and self-love. It's about approaching your relationships to your children, partners, parents, grandparents, siblings, clients, teachers, and students with empathy, kindness, compassion, grace, and nonreactivity. It's about noticing, appreciating, and being conscious of the world, of this earth and what it needs. It's about cultivating gratitude for each moment you experience, even when it feels uncomfortable.

Ultimately, mindful living gives you the chance to elevate the *being* in "human being," and this includes joys and challenges. The truth is, you can't always choose how life unfolds. However, you can choose how to respond to what unfolds. Although it's difficult, if you work on choosing a mindful lens, you bear less suffering.

You might think of it like pointillism, a painting technique in which small dots of color are applied in patterns to form an image. Formal and informal practices are the small dots. Mindful living presents opportunities to take a step back, see the entire picture, and absorb a new perspective on yourself, your relationships, and the world as a whole.

As such, the mindful living practices will look a little different from the others in this book. Sometimes there will be step-by-step instructions. Other practices will offer approaches that invite mindful living.

All of these practices are designed to be practiced for five minutes a day, yet because of the reflection they elicit, you might want to spend more time with them.

Postpractice Awareness

Each practice will begin with a quick introduction of the journey you will embark upon, and some will end with postpractice questions. At any point in this book, you may want to come back to following set of questions to deepen your awareness. I hope that you remember, even in the asking, to always maintain a gentleness toward yourself. Again, there is no right or wrong, but only increased awareness, as you consider these questions:

- How did this practice make you feel?

- What do you notice in your body after engaging in this practice? Do you feel more relaxed? If the answer is no, that's okay. The purpose is not to relax but to notice how you feel without an expectation of how you ought to feel.

- What did you notice—if anything—before, during, and after practice?

- Did you notice a desire to rush it or finish the practice sooner than intended?

- Did you feel a pull toward past- or future-oriented thinking (like a to-do list), or any other thought unrelated to the practice?

- Did any particular thoughts, emotions, or sensations come up during the practice? Remember to observe with compassion.

- Were you able to redirect your attention back to the task at hand in a nonjudgmental way?

- Do you notice any desire to judge the way you practiced?

As you answer these questions, resist the urge to judge your responses. Instead, just observe them with compassion. I also recommend keeping a Quick Calm journal, in which you can write down your answers to these postpractice awareness questions and anything else that comes up as you practice and beyond. Visit http://www.newharbinger.com/46080 to download this list of postpractice awareness questions.

Remember to validate your practice. Always! Practice is not about right or wrong. It's about showing up. After each practice, validate what you've just done by saying thank you to yourself, either out loud or in your mind. I'm also a huge fan of an *I took time out of my busy schedule* dance!

Now you practice! Remember, I am here with you through it all.

PART 2

Formal Practice

1. Diaphragmatic Breathing (Focused Attention)

This first formal practice focuses attention on the breath with diaphragmatic breathing. This way of breathing uses the diaphragm and allows for a fuller, slower, and more rhythmic breath. This technique reduces stress by breaking shallow patterns of chest-dominant breathing.

Diaphragmatic breathing is helpful because slowing down, breathing more evenly, and directing the breath into the diaphragm instead of the chest initiates a relaxation response. Also, one of the surest ways to hone our ability to pay attention is to focus on something specific, such as the breath. Ideally, you sustain your attention on the breath, but being human, your mind might wander away from it. When it does wander away, you just gently notice where your mind goes and redirect your attention back to the breath. It can be challenging to maintain focused attention on the breath, yet after repeated practice, sustained attention becomes easier. It's a process after all!

Practice

1. Set a timer for five minutes.

2. Gently close your eyes or just soften your gaze.

3. Keeping your mouth closed, take a slow deep breath in through your nostrils. While you do so, gently allow your abdomen to fill as if it were a balloon being inflated with air.

4. Hold your breath for a few moments.

5. Slowly and fully exhale through pursed lips. While exhaling, pull your abdomen back toward your spine as if it were a balloon being emptied of air.

6. After your exhale, take a few moments to pause and notice—without judgment—how you feel.

7. When you are ready, repeat the inhale and exhale in the same way as before, and begin to find your own natural rhythm of *inhale, hold...exhale. Pause. Repeat.*

8. As you get into a rhythm, notice the sensation of breathing. Feel your breath going in through your nostrils and out through pursed lips. Identify where the sensation of breathing feels most prominent.

9. Continue to sustain your attention on the movement of the inhale and the exhale.

10. Don't try too hard. Be with your breath as gently as you can. See if you can even let go of any thoughts and relax into the breath. Continue to *gently breathe in...hold...gently breathe out. Pause.*

11. If your attention wanders, just notice where it goes, and gently redirect it back to the sensation of breathing.

12. When the timer goes off, repeat the cycle one more time: *Inhale, hold…exhale. Pause.*

13. Take a moment to notice—with curiosity and without judgment—how you feel.

14. When you are ready, open your eyes slowly, if they were closed, and return to your natural gaze.

2. Body Scan

Body-centered practices, like the body scan, can help relieve stress and cultivate self-compassion, as you use your body to practice conscious, present-centered, nonjudgmental awareness. You learn to be aware of whatever sensation is arising and then learn to notice the difference between the direct experience of these sensations and the indirect perceptions and judgments that you add on to that experience.

As you narrow your focus on each detailed part of the body, you begin to nonjudgmentally identify the intricacies of what you are feeling and where you are feeling it. The body scan also allows you to train your mind to broaden its focus beyond specific body parts to an awareness of the body as a whole. This greater understanding of what your body endures allows you to see what it feels, accept the feeling, and cultivate compassion for it. This helps release and relieve stress.

Practice

1.   Set a timer for five minutes.

2.   Close your eyes or soften your gaze.

3. Awareness of breath: Gently bring your awareness to your neutral breathing. Notice where the sensations of breathing feel most prominent. Is this experience in the nostrils? In the mouth? On the tongue? Is it felt in the rising and falling of your abdomen or chest as you inhale and exhale? Just notice.

4. Entire body: Bring awareness to your entire body, as a whole, and notice the sensation of it. How does it feel? Is your body restless and tense or calm and relaxed? Notice any pain. Just observe what you feel without judgment. Noticing nothing is also noticing.

5. Head: As you continue to breathe comfortably at your own pace, shift your attention toward your head. Without judgment, see if you can detect any physical sensations arising in the back, top, or sides of your head.

6. Face: Continue to breathe comfortably, and on the next exhale bring your awareness to your face. Notice any sensation that arises. Become aware of the chin, the lips, the inside of the mouth, the tongue, the cheeks, the eyes, the eyebrows, and the ears. Observe the sensations and notice if they change, linger, or come and go.

7. Neck and throat: Continue to breathe comfortably, and on the next exhale, bring your attention to your neck and throat area. Without judgment, notice any sensations that arise. Give them your full and undivided attention. What do your neck and throat feel like? Again, if there are no sensations to notice, notice the absence.

8. Shoulders: On the next exhale, guide your attention toward your shoulders. Allow yourself to focus on any sensations there. If you experience particularly intense sensations, see if you can detect the discomfort without judgment. Try to maintain a curious stance rather than resist or fight the sensations.

9. Arms: Now you are going to explore the arms. Survey the right arm first, starting at your armpit, and make your way toward your elbow, and your wrist. Explore the front, the back, and the sides of each area. See if you can maintain a gentle curiosity as you note what sensations arise. Survey these sensations in as much detail as possible. Now repeat for the left arm.

10. Hands: Continue to breathe at a rhythm that is most comfortable for you. On your next exhale, let your attention fall upon your hands, and freely notice any sensation that comes up. Pay attention to your right hand and then your left hand. Perhaps you are experiencing tightness or maybe even tingling or pressure. Are your hands cool or warm? Observe the quality of each sensation without judging it, fighting it, or resisting it.

11. Back: On the next exhale, guide your attention to your back. There may be sensations of pain, pressure, heat, or coolness. Simply observe what you feel and know you don't have to change anything. Give yourself permission to explore and feel each sensation as it unfolds from moment to moment. Whatever you are experiencing in your lower back and surrounding areas in this moment, see if you

can welcome the sensations with compassion. See if you can lean into them without fighting or resisting.

12. Legs and feet: Mindfully shift your attention to your legs and ankles. Allow yourself to be present with each sensation. Allow yourself to be present with the right leg, from your buttock down to your thigh, past your knee, down your shin, and to the ankle, toes, sole, and heel. Next, repeat the process for the left leg.

13. Back to breath: When you are ready, bring your attention back to your breathing, noticing the inhale through your nostrils and the exhale through pursed lips.

14. When you are ready, open your eyes slowly, if they were closed, and return to your natural gaze.

3. Progressive Muscle Relaxation

Progressive muscle relaxation (PMR) entails deliberately tensing muscles and then releasing tension as you progress down your body. The concept behind this is simple: by deliberately tensing muscles and then relaxing them, you can achieve more relaxed muscles than you started with. It also helps you practice awareness of what your muscles actually feel like when they are relaxed, which is easy to forget if they are chronically clenched.

Research suggests that PMR can control even the stress response by reducing cortisol, a hormone released during the fight-or-flight response. In one study, researchers administered PMR to over a hundred first-year university students and measured cortisol secretion and self-reported stress levels a week before and a week after practice. Both levels were significantly reduced after practice, independent of age, gender, and levels of neuroticism.[17] In other words, by consciously tensing and then relaxing muscles, you can reduce your stress level.

Practice

Like most formal practice, PMR starts with the breath. You will tense each of your muscles as you inhale and relax as you exhale. For each body part, try to notice the difference between the tensed state and the relaxed state.

1. Set a timer for five minutes.

2. Find your breath. Close your eyes if it feels comfortable. Inhale gently, hold your breath, and then exhale slowly. Pause after each exhale.

3. Eyebrows: Start by raising your eyebrows as you inhale. Keep them up for approximately ten to fifteen seconds, or whatever feels comfortable for you, and then relax them and let them fall as you exhale.

4. Eyes: Close your eyes tightly as if the sun were too bright. Hold the tension for approximately ten to fifteen seconds, hold it a little longer…a little longer…and now relax the eyes. Let the tension flow out, and notice if your eyes feel any different.

5. Mouth: Widen your mouth into a smile. Hold the tension for approximately ten to fifteen seconds, hold it a little longer…a little longer…and now relax.

6. Neck: Moving down the body, tighten your neck by bringing your chin toward your chest…not too much…just enough to feel a slight tension in your neck. Hold it for approximately ten to fifteen

seconds and feel the tension…hold a little longer, and then slowly let the chin come up as you feel the tension go.

7. Arms and hands: Extend both arms out straight while making a fist. Tighten both arms from the hand to the shoulder. Feel the tension in your biceps, forearms, backs of the arms, elbows, wrists, and fingers. Hold that tension for roughly ten to fifteen seconds. Now relax. Let your arms drop and allow all of the tension to flow out. Relax your arms and notice how your biceps, forearms, backs of the arms, elbows, wrists, and fingers feel.

8. Shoulders: Raise your shoulders up toward your ears and hold them tight for approximately ten to fifteen seconds, or whatever feels comfortable for you. Then exhale and relax your shoulders.

9. Abdomen: Tighten your abdomen by pulling it in as though you wanted it to touch the back of your chair. Hold that position, feeling the tension, for about ten to fifteen seconds. Now relax, no longer pulling your abdomen in, and let your muscles soften as you exhale.

10. Legs: Slowly lift both legs, and point your toes back toward your body. Notice the tension in your thighs, knees, calves, ankles, feet, and toes. Hold that position for about ten to fifteen seconds, or whatever feels best for you. Then let go and allow your legs to relax. Notice the difference between the tension and the relaxation.

11. Feet: Turn your feet inward toward each other. Curl your toes and gently tighten them. Hold this position for roughly ten to fifteen seconds, feeling all areas of increased tension. Now relax and gently

allow your feet and toes to return to their former position on the floor.

12. Entire body: Lastly, see if you can tense your entire body. Think of your body as one stiff board. Hold and feel tension everywhere, from your eyebrows to your toes, and everywhere in between. Hold this position for approximately ten to fifteen seconds before letting go as you exhale.

13. When you are ready, open your eyes slowly if they were closed, and return to your natural gaze.

4. Autogenic Training

Autogenic training (AT) is a technique that recognizes the power of words as a means to refocus our experience. Sometimes referred to as *self-hypnosis*, AT practice entails eliciting the body's natural relaxation response using specific verbal statements about heaviness and warmth. AT was originally developed by German psychiatrist Johannes Shultz and colleagues who reported that up to 70 percent of their patients with anxiety experienced relief within a few weeks of AT practice.[18] Since its development, there have been a multitude of studies establishing AT's beneficial impact on health. An examination of data from seventy-three studies indicated that AT helped treat a diverse range of challenges, including high blood pressure, migraine, depression, and insomnia.[19]

Practice

1. Set a timer for five minutes.

2. Close your eyes or soften your gaze.

3. Start to breathe comfortably and effortlessly. Inhale through the nose, hold your breath for a moment, and then exhale slowly through pursed lips, pausing for a moment at the end of each exhale.

4. Find a breathing rhythm that feels comfortable and natural.

5. When you are ready, silently say to yourself, *I now give myself permission to relax.*

6. Now visualize your right arm. See that arm in your mind's eye, and say to yourself: *My right arm is heavy. My right arm is heavy and warm. My right arm is heavy, warm, comfortable, and relaxed.*

7. Next, visualize your left arm, and silently say to yourself: *My left arm is heavy. My left arm is heavy and warm. My left arm is heavy, warm, comfortable, and relaxed.*

8. Next, visualize both arms, and silently say to yourself: *Both arms are heavy. Both arms are heavy and warm. Both arms are heavy, warm, comfortable, and relaxed.*

9. Now visualize both of your legs, and silently say to yourself: *My legs are heavy. My legs are heavy and warm. My legs are heavy, warm, comfortable, and relaxed.*

10. Next, visualize your neck and shoulders, and silently say to yourself: *My neck and shoulders are heavy. My neck and shoulders are warm. My neck and shoulders are heavy, warm, comfortable, and relaxed.*

11. Now visualize your abdomen, and silently say to yourself: *My abdomen, which is my body's core, is warm and relaxed. My abdomen is warm and relaxed.*

12. Now visualize your heart beating, and silently say to yourself: *My heartbeat is calm. My heartbeat is calm and regular. My heartbeat is calm, regular, and relaxed.*

13. Find your breath, both the inhale and the exhale, and silently say to yourself: *My breath is calm. My breath is calm and regular. My breath is calm, regular, and relaxed.*

14. Now broaden your attention, so you visualize your neck, shoulders, arms, legs, and abdomen. Silently say to yourself: *My body, my neck, my shoulders, my arms, my legs, and my abdomen are heavy. My body, my neck, my shoulders, my arms, my legs, and my abdomen are heavy, warm, comfortable, and relaxed.*

15. Moving back up your body, visualize your forehead, and silently say to yourself: *My forehead is cool. My forehead is cool, comfortable, and relaxed.*

16. Next, envision your entire body from a bird's-eye view, and silently say to yourself: *My body is calm. My body is calm, comfortable, and relaxed.*

17. When you are ready, open your eyes slowly if they were closed, and return to your natural gaze.

5. Guided Imagery

The general premise of guided imagery (GI) is to intentionally invoke mental images—real or made-up—using words or sounds, with the goal of shifting our attention toward the present moment. This practice will focus on honing your ability to notice different sensations as they unfold in your mind.

GI has been well studied across many different cultures. Research has indicated GI's benefits in many areas of wellness, including increasing creativity, more effective problem solving, and stress reduction.[20] In one study, GI was shown to significantly decrease salivary cortisol levels when compared with a control group that did not participate in GI practice.[21]

Guided imagery can be tailored to fit any aspect of your life. To be most beneficial, it transports you to a safe and captivating space using all of your accessible senses. (Note: If any of your senses are compromised or if you experience synesthesia, GI might feel particularly overwhelming. Please proceed with caution, and consider using this exercise while in the care of a professional, or feel free to skip it altogether.)

Practice

1. Set a timer for five minutes.

2. Close your eyes or soften your gaze.

3. Take a slow deep breath in, hold it for a moment, and then exhale slowly and fully through pursed lips. Take a moment to pause before the next inhale.

4. Start by imagining a new lightness in your being. Imagine you have no pressures, no worries, and no responsibility to anyone or anything. All you are asked to do is notice.

5. Take another slow deep breath in, hold it for a moment, and then exhale slowly and fully through pursed lips. As you exhale, let your shoulders come down away from your ears, allow your arms to fall beside you in your lap, and let yourself lean into whatever you're sitting or lying on.

6. Imagine you are walking somewhere outdoors—a real location or somewhere you dream up. Think of a soothing and safe space. Perhaps it's a beach, a mountainside landscape, a park, or a street in your favorite city.

7. It is a beautiful day. Look up and notice the sky. The sky is breathtakingly blue, a deep, beautiful shade. Focus on the blue sky.

8. Take a nice deep breath in through the nose, hold for a few moments, and exhale through pursed lips. At the end of the exhale, pause for a moment before the next inhale.

9. Notice the emergence of fluffy white clouds. Can you take a closer look to see their texture? Take a moment to watch them move across the blue sky, slowly swaying and changing shape but never blocking the sun. What shapes do you notice? Say them to yourself.

10. Take another deep breath in through the nose and fill the diaphragm. Hold it for a moment before gently and slowly exhaling through pursed lips.

11. Take a pause, and in that moment see if you can feel enveloped by a sense of peace and tranquility as you allow yourself to feel the warmth of the sun on your skin. How does it feel? Just notice.

12. Notice the ground underneath your feet as you continue your walk in this landscape. Is it grass? Sand? Concrete? Rocks? Notice your weight being held by the ground. You are grounded in your terrain. Take a moment to pause wherever you are standing in the scene.

13. Wherever you are grounded, turn your attention toward sound. Do you hear water running? Waves crashing? Cars buzzing? Are there animals making sounds around you? Birds? Crickets? Notice, and let the sound envelop you without judging it. Name the sounds out loud if you'd like.

14. Stand still for a few more moments, and feel the sun, the air, and perhaps a breeze across your skin as you continue to listen.

15. Breathe in slowly and gently, and exhale slowly and fully through pursed lips. Take a moment to pause.

16. Then, as you walk further along in your scene, allow your mind to wander with a sense of freedom. There is nothing you must do other than be in this soothing outdoor landscape, on your own terms.

17. Once you've allowed your mind to wander as it wishes, refocus your gaze toward the horizon. The sun is beginning to set slowly and steadily. It is one of those brilliant sunsets, full of different shades of pink, purple, and maybe even a touch of orange. The colors move in a beautiful pattern as the bright blue sky becomes softer and supple.

18. As the sun slowly leaves the horizon, see if you can allow yourself to surrender to a quiet joy, comfort, and peace.

19. When you feel comfortable, take a slow deep breath in through the nose. Then exhale slowly and fully through pursed lips. Take a moment to pause.

20. When you are ready, open your eyes slowly, if they were closed, and return to your natural gaze.

6. Rooting

Rooting is a practice that grounds the body in safety and stability. Finding this present-moment awareness, rooted with your feet firmly planted on the ground, is especially helpful when the mind is ruminating. This rooting practice also helps with your posture by aligning the skeleton and bringing it back to a neutral place, which is especially important if you tend to be hunched over a laptop or other device for many hours a day. Figure 1 illustrates the rooting yoga pose called *tadasana*, or mountain pose.

Figure 1. Tadasana

As you align and allow your vertebrae to stack one on top of the other, your core begins to strengthen. This posturing opens up your chest and makes room for your heart, lungs, and other internal organs so that deep diaphragmatic breathing (see practice 1) becomes more possible.

Research indicates that this practice reduces back and hip pain. It also helps regulate the digestive, nervous, and respiratory systems.[22]

It is best to do this practice with bare feet.

Practice

1. Set a timer for five minutes.

2. Stand or sit, whichever you prefer, with your feet hip-width apart and flat on the floor.

3. Keep your eyes open and look straight ahead.

4. Allow your arms to rest gently at your sides, palms facing in and gently touching your thighs.

5. Take three full breaths, gently inhaling through the nose and exhaling deeply through pursed lips (see practice 1 if needed).

6. On your fourth inhale, lift your toes off the floor momentarily, spread them apart, and then lower them back onto the floor.

7. As you exhale, feel your weight evenly balanced in both feet, from the toes to the balls of your feet.

8. Check in with yourself and see if you feel balanced.

9. Adjust your head so that your chin is parallel to the floor.

10. Gently lift your body, from the knees upward, and tuck your tail-bone slightly under your spine, as you align your hips directly over the ankles.

11. On your next inhale, breathe into and fill your diaphragm, allowing the waist to expand ever so slightly, and press the crown of your head up toward the ceiling.

12. As you exhale, drop the shoulders down, bring your abdomen in toward your spine, and reach your fingertips toward the floor.

13. Gently move your shoulders back as you open your chest.

14. Check in with your body to make sure you are not putting too much weight on your toes or your heels; you don't want to be leaning forward nor falling backward.

15. Look straight ahead with a relaxed gaze.

16. Relax your throat, jaw, and facial muscles.

17. With each inhale, see if you can feel your spine lift ever so subtly.

18. With each exhale, roll your shoulders back, and bring your abdomen toward your spine to open your chest.

19. When five minutes are up, take one last full inhale and exhale, and slowly come out of the posture to a regular standing or seated position.

7. Rectangle Breathing

This exercise uses the principles of diaphragmatic breathing (see practice 1) with a counting element. The counting element helps to pace and regulate breathing, which can become more erratic during stressful periods. Since the heart rate naturally goes down on each exhale, exhaling (on a count of eight) for twice as long as the inhale (a count of four) for a few minutes allows you to slow down your physiology and elicit the relaxation response. Pausing for another eight seconds after the exhale keeps you from jumping right into the next inhale. This pause allows you to notice how you feel after each breath cycle without an expectation of how you ought to feel.

This practice incorporates imagery to help focus your attention toward the present moment (see practice 5). If you find it hard to count to yourself and visualize in your mind's eye at the same time, then it's okay to just count.

Practice

1. Set a timer for five minutes.

2. Gently close your eyes or soften your gaze.

3. Keeping your mouth closed, take a slow deep breath in through your nostrils. While you do so, count to yourself: *In, two, three, four.*

4. Hold your breath while counting to yourself: *Hold, two, three, four.*

5. Then slowly and fully exhale through pursed lips as you count to yourself: *Out, two, three, four, five, six, seven, eight.*

6. After your exhale take a brief pause and count to yourself: *Pause, two, three, four, five, six, seven, eight.*

7. Repeat all of the previous steps two more times.

8. Now, incorporate a visual exercise. As you inhale and count to four, imagine the left side of a rectangle being drawn.

9. As you hold your breath for a count of four, imagine the right side of the rectangle being drawn.

10. As you slowly exhale to a count of eight, imagine the top of the rectangle being drawn from left to right, connecting the tops of the two sides.

11. As you pause for a count of eight, imagine the bottom of the rectangle being drawn from left to right to complete the rectangle.

12. Repeat steps 8 through 11 until the timer is up.

13. If the timer rings and you have just started a breathing cycle, don't stop until you have finished your pause at the end of the cycle.

14. When you are ready, open your eyes slowly, if they were closed, and return to your natural gaze.

8. Loving-Kindness Meditation

Loving-kindness meditation (LKM) is a mindfulness-based practice geared toward eliciting unconditional states of kindness and compassion for self and others. This practice has three components: generating compassion for self, compassion for someone you care about, and compassion for all beings. It is a practice that connects you to yourself, to those in your life, and to the entire universe. Although more research into the efficacy of LKM is needed, there are emerging studies that support its benefits to well-being. A study in the *Harvard Review of Psychology* speaks to its usefulness in the treatment of chronic pain.[23] Another study found preliminary benefits for those experiencing social anxiety, anger, and stress related to long-term caregiving.[24] There are even initial neuroimaging studies that point to LKM's ability to enhance the activation of brain areas associated with empathy and emotional processing.[25]

While nurturing compassion is also part of mindful living (see practice 24), this is an opportunity to practice compassion in a more formal way.

Practice

1. Set a timer for five minutes.

2. Set a timer for five minutes.

3. Gently close your eyes or soften your gaze.

4. Find the natural rhythm of your breath and spend a few moments with it.

5. When you're ready, think of a person you care about.

6. Take a deep breath in, hold it, and then slowly exhale.

7. During the pause at the end of the exhale, silently repeat the following statements, inserting the name of the person you're thinking about: *May this person feel loved. May this person's suffering come to an end. May this person feel contentment and compassion. May this person feel at peace.*

8. Take a moment to find your breath, fully inhaling, holding, and then exhaling slowly and gently.

9. At the end of the exhale, find your pause, and say silently to yourself: *May I feel loved. May my suffering come to an end. May I feel contentment and compassion. May I feel at peace.*

10. Next, take a full inhale, hold, and exhale slowly and gently.

11. At the end of the exhale, find your pause, and say silently to yourself: *May the whole world feel loved. May the whole world's suffering come to an end. May the whole world feel contentment and compassion. May the whole world feel at peace.*

12. Again, take a moment to find your breath, hold it, and exhale slowly and gently.

13. Repeat the entire practice or each separate component as many times as you can until five minutes are up.

14. Remember to end with a full inhale, hold, and gentle exhale. Finish with a pause.

15. Without judgment, take a moment to notice how you feel.

16. When you are ready, open your eyes slowly, if they were closed, and return to your natural gaze.

9.   Grounding

Grounding in your five senses is one of the surest ways to connect back to the present moment. When not grounded in your present experience, you are likely to be distracted by the projections of your mind. Engaging with your senses can help regulate emotions sometimes elicited by racing thoughts, which create stories that are unhelpful and that don't serve your ultimate well-being. This exercise helps you focus on the external environment by noting sensory experiences outside of your own thoughts and sensations.

Note: If you have challenges with any of your senses, please do whatever part of the exercise that feels right to you. If you have trouble hearing, for example, double up on one of the other senses. If you experience ringing in your ears, or a whooshing sound from hearing aids, see if you can notice any other sounds beyond the ones you are used to. If not, can you notice the sounds with compassion and tune in to them without judgment? If you find this too triggering because of the challenges, it is okay to skip this exercise.

Practice

1.   Set a timer for five minutes.

2. Slow your breath with a deep inhale, filling your diaphragm like a balloon. Hold your breath for a few moments, and then release it with a slow and gentle exhale through pursed lips.

3. At the end of the exhale, find a pause.

4. Continue to breathe at a pace that feels natural to you.

5. As you continue to breathe naturally, become aware of five things that you can see. You can start with the more obvious objects or people, but then see if you can go deeper and see the subtle things in the space around you.

6. For each thing you notice, silently describe it to yourself in one sentence (for example, *I see my dog curled up on the blue chair*).

7. Take a deep breath in through your nose and hold it momentarily. Then exhale through pursed lips and pause.

8. Next, become aware of four things you can hear. Start with the most obvious, and then see if you can hone in on more subtle sounds (*I hear the noise the air conditioning makes*).

9. Just notice these sounds without judgment. The sounds are neither good nor bad, right nor wrong, even if it's loud honking. They are just there to take in.

10. Take a deep breath in through the nose, and hold it momentarily. Then exhale through pursed lips, and pause.

11. Next, pay attention to three things you can feel or touch. Start with something neutral outside yourself. For example, can you feel your pillow? A blanket? The clothing you are wearing?

12. Take a deep breath in through the nose, and hold it momentarily. Then exhale through pursed lips, and pause.

13. Now see if you can smell two things. If smells are less obvious, bring your hand toward your nose to perhaps smell the lotion you applied earlier in the day. What else can you smell, as subtle as it might be? Simply notice it without judging it.

14. Take a deep breath in through the nose, and hold it momentarily. Then exhale through pursed lips, and pause.

15. Finally, find one thing you can taste. Maybe it's something left over from your last meal, maybe it's the mint from your toothpaste, maybe it's from a cup of coffee. If you can't connect with a taste right in this moment, think of the last flavor you remember. Simply notice it without judging it.

16. Take a deep breath in through the nose, and hold it momentarily. Then exhale through pursed lips, and pause.

17. Repeat this practice as many times as possible until five minutes are up. Each time, see if you can challenge yourself to find new things to sense, if possible.

10. Receptive Attention

In the diaphragmatic breathing (focused attention) practice (see practice 1), you practiced sustaining your attention upon something very specific, the breath. When you were challenged by your wandering mind, you noticed where your mind went, and without judgment redirected your attention back to the breath to keep honing your focus.

Now, this exercise helps cultivate your attention so that it's broad enough to be receptive to your entire field of awareness. For example, you start your practice focusing on the breath and then you notice the birds chirping. Instead of redirecting back to the breath, you focus on the chirping. If you are focusing on the chirping, and a thought comes to mind, you learn to just notice the thought, without judging it or engaging with it. Broadening your focus in this way helps you take a step back and bear witness to your internal and external experiences with more compassion.

Note: This might feel difficult, and that's okay. Feel free to continue this practice without judgment or just switch back to focused attention on your breath (see practice 1) whenever you'd like.

Practice

1. Set a timer for five minutes.

2. Gently close your eyes or soften your gaze.

3. Find the rhythm of your breath and settle into a pace that feels most comfortable for you.

4. Next, begin to notice whatever it is that comes into your conscious awareness. This might be the feeling of your own heartbeat, the sound of something in the background, or even thoughts about your to-do list.

5. Simply notice as if through the eyes of a loving witness.

6. Now allow for other sensations, thoughts, and feelings to come into your realm of attention.

7. This might be an ache in the neck, a sensation of hunger, a thought about a conversation you had yesterday, or even a feeling, like worry.

8. See if you can notice it, even if it feels charged. Instead of engaging with it, labeling it good or bad, or judging and expanding on it (*Here I go again with that ruminating*), just allow yourself to note it.

9. Keep noticing and focusing on the process (*I am having a thought*) of what comes up in your conscious realm of attention, instead of the content (*I'm thinking about this annoying conversation over and over again*). You can repeat *I am having a thought* or *I am having a feeling* as many times as you need.

10. Try to watch with compassion and nonjudgment any tendencies that come up, taking them at face value. Whether it's a tendency to escape a certain feeling or sensation, a desire to end this exercise, or even an urge to go down a rabbit hole of thinking (*That conversation reminds me of how bad my job is*), see if you can continue to bear witness as if you were a distant bystander watching a kaleidoscope of different experiences going through your mind.

11. Continue to observe, and if you do start to judge, evaluate, or label, notice that too without judgment. See if you can redirect toward the stance of a more neutral witness.

12. Do this for as long as you are able, and then when you are ready, find your breath.

13. Inhale through your nose, hold your breath for a few moments, and then slowly and fully exhale through pursed lips. Then take a pause.

14. Take a few more diaphragmatic breaths.

15. Be with your breath as gently as you can, and see if you can even relax into your breathing. There is no right or wrong way to do this. Just gently breathe in…hold…gently breathe out…pause.

16. When you are ready, open your eyes slowly, if they were closed, and return to your natural gaze.

PART 3

Informal Practice

11. Mindful Waking

A new day is theoretically full of potential. It is an opportunity to move toward personal and professional goals, and it offers a renewed chance to show up for yourself and loved ones with even more compassion and love. Yet all the newness falls by the wayside as you engage in the same jolting awake-snooze cycle until you finally give in to the call to action to get out of bed and begin the day's journey. This often primes you for anxiety, right upon waking in the morning.

Waking up more mindfully can help offset anxiety. Practicing this regularly will help you consciously start your day so that you are less vulnerable to stressors along the way that might otherwise overwhelm you. You are also likely to experience more efficient focus, greater productivity, and greater overall calmness throughout your day.

Setup

- Wake up as gently as possible.

- Don't set a timer for this exercise, but allow yourself approximately five minutes, or whatever feels right.

Practice

1. Upon first waking, gently notice the feeling of your body coming back into conscious awareness. Notice how your arms and feet are naturally positioned as you lie in bed.

2. Put your hand on your heart as you scan your entire body and, without judgment, observe any sensations that arise.

3. When you are ready, prop up your pillows and gently come to a comfortable seated position. Notice what it was like to go from lying down to sitting. What, if anything, do you observe?

4. Then, take three diaphragmatic breaths (see practice 1), breathing in through your nose and out through pursed lips.

5. Ask yourself the question *What is my intention for the day?*

6. If you're having trouble finding an intention to set, ask yourself: *What quality of my mind do I want to strengthen and develop? What do I need to do in order to take better care of myself? How can I approach my relationship with myself and others with more compassion? What would help me feel more fulfilled?*

7. Now create one present-tense intentional statement. For example, if you want to feel calmer and more present for yourself and others, then your intention might be: *I am calm. I am present for myself and those I care about.*

8. Repeat your intention out loud three times with a deep breath after each recitation.

9. When you are ready, gently swing your legs to the side of the bed so that your feet touch the ground.

10. Spend a moment grounding your feet on the floor. Feel your weight evenly balanced in both feet, from your toes to your heels.

11. Take a deep breath and, as you exhale gently and slowly, come to a standing position.

12. Again, feel your weight evenly balanced in both feet from your toes to your heels.

13. Take a moment to notice what it was like to go from lying down, to sitting, and ultimately to standing.

14. Repeat your intention out loud again three times, with a deep breath after each recitation.

15. After the last exhale, validate your practice. A thank-you to yourself can go a long way.

Increasing Your Awareness

After practicing mindful waking for several mornings, ask yourself:

- How has setting intentions for my day affected my relationship with myself and others?

- How has repeating this practice affected the way the rest of my day unfolds?

- Did I notice a difference in my ability to handle stressors during the day? Did I notice a shift in my mood?

There are no right answers, only exploration and learning.

12. Mindful Toothbrushing

Brushing our teeth is something most of us do twice a day, day after day. This repetition makes brushing a habitual act and, therefore, commonly done on autopilot. Being on autopilot, especially if you are getting ready for work, also makes rumination more likely. Before you know it, your teeth are brushed, but you've already mentally gone through your day's to-do list, maybe even thought about how you are going to tackle an overflowing inbox. This is a primer for stress—before you've even left the bathroom. I like to say, "Don't suffer twice." If work is stressful, it will be stressful. Anticipating work will be stressful, doubles the stress.

This practice of mindful toothbrushing will help you begin the day with conscious, purposeful attention on a task that has, more likely than not, become a habitual act you do with little awareness. It might even help reduce the unnecessary stress that ruminating on your upcoming day can bring. You might even learn to savor the experience.

Setup

- Enter the bathroom where you keep your toothbrush.

- Set a timer for five minutes.

Practice

1. Ground your feet on the floor, and notice how it feels to be standing after a night of sleeping or after a long day of moving around. What does the floor feel like under your feet? If you are barefoot, does the floor feel cold or warm? Just notice.

2. Bring your attention to your breath and take three diaphragmatic breaths (see practice 1).

3. If you'd like, gently splash some warm water on your face, and notice how it feels.

4. Take one more diaphragmatic breath as you wipe your face dry.

5. Notice the experience of extending your arm toward your toothbrush. What hand do you naturally and instinctually use to grab it? How does it feel in your hand? Is it light or heavy?

6. Keep looking at the toothbrush as you hold it. What color is it? Is it clean, or is there dry toothpaste on it from previous brushing? What do the bristles look like? Just notice without judgment.

7. Now bring your attention to your mouth, teeth, and tongue. What do they feel like before brushing? Describe this to yourself.

8. Turn on the water to wet your brush. What does the water look like when it ricochets off the bristles? After you've noticed, turn off the water with awareness.

9. Take the tube of toothpaste, and squeeze out a pea-size amount onto the bristles. Replace the cap, and put the tube down gently. What does the toothpaste look like? What color is it? What does it smell like? Notice if the toothbrush feels heavier in your hand with the toothpaste.

10. Notice as you extend your arm toward your mouth to begin brushing. What muscles do you feel working?

11. First brush the outside of the bottom teeth, then the inside.

12. Then brush the outside of the upper teeth, then the inside.

13. If at any time you have to spit out excess toothpaste and foam, do so. Then rinse with water, and continue brushing.

14. If at any time during the exercise your mind wanders, just bring your attention back to the task at hand, without judging your thoughts.

15. Brush your tongue, if you'd like, with the same mindful awareness you gave to your teeth. Does brushing these different textures feel differently?

16. When you are done, turn on the water, extend your arm away from your mouth, and rinse your brush. Then rinse your mouth.

17. Maintain your awareness as you return your toothbrush to its holder.

18. Notice how you feel. Without any judgment or expectations, observe how your entire mouth feels from your teeth to your lips to your tongue. Does it feel fresh? Clean? Notice and savor by lingering momentarily on the feeling, if you'd like to.

19. Notice your feet again as they are grounded on the floor, and take a diaphragmatic inhale and exhale.

20. Validate your practice.

Increasing Your Awareness

- Were you able to focus on brushing your teeth with mindful awareness? Just notice, without judgment.

- Did you feel a pull toward past- or future-oriented thinking or any other thought unrelated to brushing your teeth?

- If so, where did your thoughts go? Try to observe with compassion.

- Did you notice any desire to judge the way you practiced? Just note if you did, and remind yourself that there is no right or wrong way to practice.

13. Mindful Coffee Time

Many people I know relish a cup of coffee or tea in the morning so much that they go to sleep looking forward to it! Just like brushing your teeth, this is a keystone habit, which makes it easy to adapt as a mindfulness exercise. And imagine how much more you might enjoy it! Let's see if you can start your day off with more awareness of this timeless ritual.

Setup

- Make a cup of coffee or tea.

- Find a spot that is comfortable, cozy, and as quiet as possible.

- If you are used to watching or reading the morning news with your coffee or tea, see if you can set that aside just for now.

- Set a timer for five minutes.

Practice

1. As you hold the cup in hand, first feel the seat beneath you, and notice whether it's a cushioned or hard surface. Lean in and relax into it.

2. Roll your shoulders down and let the tension melt.

3. Inhale through your nose, hold for a few moments, and then exhale through pursed lips. At the end of the exhale, find a pause in your breath.

4. During this pause, begin to grasp the mug with two hands, and notice how that feels. Is the cup heavy? Do your hands feel warm from the mug ? Just notice.

5. Bring the mug down so that you can see inside it. What color is the coffee? Maybe it's black, or maybe it's light brown, if you add milk, cream, or a nondairy alternative.

6. Consider closing your eyes for this next step. Put your nose close to the lip of the mug and smell the coffee's aroma. What do you notice?

7. Take this moment to inhale again through your nose, hold for a few moments, and then exhale through pursed lips. At the end of the exhale, find a pause.

8. During the pause, slowly and methodically bring the mug to your mouth and let it graze your lips.

9. Take a sip and let it linger in your mouth before you swallow. Notice the taste. Is it bitter? Is it sweet? Is it strong? Is it weak?

10. Swallow and notice how the liquid feels going down your throat.

11. Inhale again through your nose, hold for a few moments, and then exhale through pursed lips. At the end of the exhale, find a pause.

12. After the pause, take a moment to notice any thoughts, feelings, or sensations that come up while engaging in this practice. Simply let them enter your consciousness and refrain from ruminating on them.

13. Repeat the previous steps until the timer goes off, but feel free to proceed until you finish the entire mug!

14. Validate your practice.

Increasing Your Awareness

- Were you able to focus on drinking your coffee or tea with mindful awareness? Did you notice the desire to rush the experience? Again just notice without judgment.

- Did you feel a pull toward past- or future-oriented thinking or any other thought unrelated to the task at hand? Observe with compassion.

- Did you notice any desire to judge the way you practiced? See if you can note that, and then remind yourself that practice has no expectations.

14. Mindful Showering

Your shower or bath time may be spent ruminating on past or present conversations, the things you have to accomplish during the day, or brainstorming your next big idea. Or you may go on autopilot and, in the process of showering, sometimes forget whether or not you've actually shampooed yet! This practice is aimed at reclaiming this time by consciously and purposefully paying attention and leaning into the experience as it unfolds in the moment. In this way, it won't be something you "have to do." Rather, it will be an experience that can help reduce stress and maybe even elicit relaxation. This practice is for taking a shower but can be adapted for taking a bath.

Setup

- Make sure your towel and toiletries are where you want them.

- Undress and place your clothes in the hamper or where they will stay dry.

- You can choose to use a timer for five minutes or just practice throughout the duration of your shower.

- If you do set a timer, place it in a safe and accessible area in your bathroom.

Practice

1. Before turning on the water, notice the following without judgment: your breath, any points of tension or discomfort in your body, any thoughts or emotions you may be experiencing.

2. Then notice as you bring your hand to the faucet, and consciously turn on the water to your preferred temperature. As you gauge the temperature, notice how the water feels as it hits your hand, and whether it's too hot or cold or just right. Adjust the temperature and water pressure if needed.

3. Then, step into the shower slowly and safely, and feel the floor under your feet.

4. Before putting your head under the shower, take a nice deep breath in through your nose, hold for a moment, and exhale through pursed lips. Find a pause.

5. Set an intention in your mind to attune to this experience.

6. As you step further into the shower water, notice how it feels—the temperature and pressure—on your face and the rest of your body. Watch the steam rise. How does it feel to be in the shower?

7. See if you can notice what the water sounds like. Does it sound different on different parts of your body?

8. Begin your regular washing routine.

9. As you proceed through your routine, notice the smell of each product you use: the shampoo, conditioner, soap, and so on. Breathe in the aroma of each, noticing it and the feeling it elicits.

10. Place the bath products in your hand and notice the texture of each. If you are using a washcloth or a sponge, notice the texture of it as well.

11. Begin to consciously lather your hair or body and maintain awareness of each movement. What does it feel like? Is it tingly? Refreshing? Neutral?

12. Notice how your body looks as it is being washed and any sensation that's elicited in any part of your body at any given moment, without judgment.

13. Bring your attention to your skin or hair as you rinse off. How does your skin or hair feel after using a product?

14. Notice again how the water feels against your skin as you are rinsing.

15. As your shower nears an end, maintain an overall awareness of yourself in relation to all that just transpired.

16. Turn off the water in the same way you turned it on, consciously.

17. Take a gentle, safe step out of the shower, and find your towel.

18. Now bring your attention to the feel of the dry towel on each distinct body part. See if you can dry each body part with conscious attention. Notice the feel of your now-dry clean skin.

19. Continue to notice any scents that linger or the steam still in the air.

20. Again, take a nice deep breath in through your nose, hold for a moment, and exhale through pursed lips. Find a pause.

21. Validate your experience and practice.

Increasing Your Awareness

- See if you can describe in a few words what this experience was like. You may want to write about it in your journal.

- Check in with yourself. Do you notice any changes in points of tension or differences in the intensity of thoughts or emotions you might have been experiencing before the shower? There is no right or wrong answer.

- Did you catch your mind wandering during the shower? If so, where did it go? This exploration is not about judging where it went; it's about increasing awareness.

- If your mind did wander—and chances are it did, because that's what human minds do—were you able to gently redirect your attention back to conscious washing or the sensation of water on your body?

15. Mindful Eating

Without realizing it, it's easy to ingest food without paying attention to how you are eating and what you are consuming. This makes it hard for your brain to register your satiety. Mindful eating speaks to being mindful of both what and how you eat. Paying attention to what you put into your mouth protects you from choosing foods that don't serve your overall well-being. Paying attention to how you put food into your mouth reduces your stress hormones and gives your body the time and space it needs to thoroughly digest and note your fullness.

Mindless eating can wreak havoc on your digestive abilities by eliciting stress hormones and therefore can add pounds, take away pleasure, and maintain functional gastrointestinal difficulties. In addition to reducing stress hormones, mindful eating enables you to slowly and sensually savor the action of eating, creating an experience to delight in. It also allows you to engage with your inner sense of satiety, which helps curb the overeating that leaves you feeling uncomfortable.[26]

In 2014, Khan and Zadeh studied the relationship between mindful eating and mental well-being.[27] After surveying 309 participants, results indicated a significant positive correlation between mindful eating scores and mental well-being scores.

Setup

- Use this exercise while eating a snack or a meal.

- Find a place to sit alone in a relatively quiet location for this meal. No standing and eating!

- Allow yourself this time to only eat. Don't eat in front of the phone, television, computer, or even a newspaper.

- Set a timer for five minutes or more.

Practice

1. Ask: Sit down and begin this practice by asking yourself these questions: *Why am I eating now? Am I hungry or craving something else? What am I eating now? Will this choice serve my wellness in some way?* There are no right or wrong answers. It's just a matter of noticing without judgment. Feel free to write the answers down in a journal.

2. Be grateful: Before you lean into whatever it is you are going to consume, take a moment to reflect on how grateful you are for being able to engage in this meal. You can just say, "I am grateful for this meal," or expand further as you wish.

3. Breathe: Inhale through your nose, hold for a moment, and exhale slowly and gently through pursed lips. At the end of the exhale, come to a pause.

4. Observe: When you are ready, observe the food in front of you with a sense of curiosity, almost as if you had never seen this food before. Notice the shape, the size, and the color. Do the colors look appetizing? Vibrant?

5. Be aware: At this point, and again throughout the practice, notice any urges to rush through this practice and dive into eating. See if you can observe what that feels like, and then redirect your attention back to your senses.

6. Breathe: Inhale through the nose, hold for a moment, and exhale slowly and gently through pursed lips. At the end of the exhale, come to a pause.

7. Sense: When you are ready, see if you can attune to how the food smells. You can bring the plate closer to your nose. If there are multiple things on the plate, is one aroma more dominant? Is there a subtle aroma that you wouldn't have noticed unless you really leaned into your senses? See what happens if you take a deep breath and then come back to the smell. Did anything change? Just notice.

8. Pick up the food: If you are using a fork or spoon, first note how the utensil feels in your hand. Is it heavy? Is it cold? Then as you pick up the food with your utensil, how does the additional weight feel in your hand? If you aren't using a utensil, how does the food itself feel in your hand? Is it soft or hard? Is it warm or cold?

9. Put the food in your mouth: Put one small piece of food in your mouth. Before chewing, take the time to notice how it feels on your tongue. Notice the shape, the texture, the temperature, and the flavor of the first bite.

10. Chew: Begin chewing really slowly and methodically, noticing each sensation of your teeth interacting with the food. Notice how the texture changes. Does the food become softer? Notice if the flavors change the more you chew. Keep chewing. Chew more, and notice more!

11. Swallow: After you've sufficiently chewed, so the food is broken down and easily digestible, swallow the bite. What is the experience of swallowing like? What does it feel like for the food to move down your throat and down your esophagus?

12. Notice: What did you notice as you swallowed your first bite? Is there an aftertaste in your mouth? Is there an immediate urge to dive into the next bite? Just notice.

13. Breathe: Inhale again through the nose, hold for a moment, and exhale slowly and gently through pursed lips. At the end of the exhale, come to a pause.

14. Repeat: Repeat the practice until the buzzer goes off, or continue for as long as you'd like as you engage in your meal.

15. Afterward, thank yourself for eating mindfully.

Increasing Your Awareness

- Without judging, what came up for you during this exercise? Was it helpful in any way? Did you taste your food in a different way? Was any part of mindful eating uncomfortable? Just notice.

- Did you notice any impatience or an urge to eat more quickly?

- Did you question why you were practicing mindful eating in the first place? Did this questioning last the entire time, or did it pass as you concentrated more on eating?

16. Mindful Dishwashing

The Buddhist monk and Nobel Prize–nominee Thich Nhat Hanh writes about and encourages the practice of mindful dishwashing. As he puts it, "There are two ways to wash the dishes. The first is to wash the dishes in order to have clean dishes, and the second is to wash the dishes to wash the dishes."[28] He expresses the essence of mindfully washing dishes (being fully present to this routine task) and notes the pleasure that can be found in the seemingly mundane.

In a recent study from Florida State University, researchers asked fifty-one students to wash dishes mindfully by focusing on the smell of the soap, the temperature of the water, and the feel of the dishes.[29] After mindful dishwashing, participants reported a 27 percent decrease in nervousness and a 25 percent increase in mental inspiration. These results were compared with a control group, which didn't report any benefits.

The goal of this practice is to bring attention to the present moment and the process of washing dishes while gently setting aside the end goal of having the dishes done. Perhaps the next time you bemoan that it's your turn to wash the dishes, you can remind yourself that doing it mindfully will boost your overall well-being.

Setup

- Stand in front of the sink with your usual dishwashing tools.

- Set a timer for five minutes.

Practice

1. Before turning on the water or prepping your sponge, see if you can ground your feet on the floor and feel a sense of that steadiness while you stand.

2. Without judgment, notice any tension in your body.

3. Take a few deep breaths, and just notice the sensation of the inhale through the nose and the exhale through pursed lips. Take three full deep breaths and just notice.

4. Observe the dishes you are about to wash. What do they look like? Are there different kinds of pots and pans or plates and glasses in the sink? How do they look with remnants of food on them?

5. Notice any thoughts and judgments that may arise, even if those thoughts are to avoid the task at hand. Then gently bring your attention back to the dishes in front of you. If you don't notice any thoughts, feelings, or sensations arising, that's okay, too.

6. Turn on the faucet, and gauge the temperature. Bring your attention to the way the temperature of the water feels on your hands.

7. Take the sponge in your hand and feel its texture before and after you wet it and again after you apply soap. What does it feel like in your hands?

8. Begin to wash the dishes one at a time, with a conscious awareness of every stroke of the sponge and the play of the water on the dish. Bring awareness to the movement of your hands. How do your hands feel? Do you need to scrub lighter because you are tensing your muscles?

9. Observe the dishes getting cleaner.

10. Continue to bring intention to your scrubbing and rinsing of each individual dish, all the while taking note of any adjustments you need to make so your body doesn't tense.

11. As you finish cleaning a dish, place it in the drying rack with conscious attention. How does it feel to notice the transition from dirty to clean? Repeat this step for every dish and utensil.

12. When you notice your mind wandering, gently bring it back to the dish in your hand.

13. Continue with this practice for five minutes, or until the remainder of the dishes are washed.

14. Once your practice is completed, wash your own hands mindfully. Notice the temperature and feel of the water. Observe how the soap feels between your palms and fingers, the scent of the soap, and bring your awareness to the sensation of having clean hands.

15. Validate your experience and practice. Check in with yourself and notice if there have been any changes in your body, mood, or thoughts.

Increasing Your Awareness

• Did you catch your mind wandering at all while doing this practice? If so, where did it go? This is not about judging where it went. It's about awareness.

• If your mind wandered, were you able to gently redirect your attention back to the conscious washing of the dishes?

• Did you notice any points of tension in your body when you were scrubbing each dish? Did you notice your feet getting tired? Were you able to make appropriate adjustments?

17. Mindful Sweeping

Most of us don't like doing chores, but we do them anyway. As a result, we tend to rush through them with little joy and much moaning and groaning.

There is likely a long list of more exciting things you would rather be doing than cleaning up! But doing a chore like sweeping is actually an excellent opportunity to practice mindfulness. The repetitiveness of sweeping can lend itself to dullness and getting lost in the unhelpful aspects of wandering mind. This practice will help you find meaning in the mundane, take you out of autopilot's grip, and reap the benefits of mindfulness practice.

Setup

- Mentally note where the broom resides.

- Set a timer for five minutes.

Practice

1. Before starting, see if you can ground your feet on the floor and feel a sense of steadiness as you stand.

2. Take a few deep breaths and notice the sensation of the inhale through your nose and the exhale through pursed lips. Take three full deep breaths.

3. Notice each step you take toward wherever the broom resides. Walk toward it with intention and purpose.

4. Extend your arm toward the broom's handle and notice how it feels. What is the texture of the handle like in your hand? Is it made of wood, metal, plastic? Is it smooth or rough? Notice how you grip the handle as you prepare to sweep. Which hand is on top of the other? Is the grip particularly loose or tight? Just observe.

5. Before you start to sweep, look at the floor and notice it with curiosity. Do you see dust? Other kinds of dirt? Without judging or labeling, observe what it looks like and what it looks like compared with other areas of the floor.

6. Start to sweep intentionally. Sweep in one direction. Sweep again, maybe reaching to a further spot on the floor. Reach and sweep, reach and sweep. Take steps as necessary to cover the area you are sweeping. Notice the broom bringing the dust and dirt on the floor into one pile.

7. Repeat step 6, but this time, as you sweep, say out loud "sweep" as you do it.

8. Keep doing this until you have a pile on the floor, and then start to intentionally sweep the pile into a dustpan. How does the

collection of dust and dirt look in the dustpan compared with how it looked on the floor?

9. Intentionally place the broom down for a moment. Bring the dustpan toward the garbage can.

10. Take one diaphragmatic breath (see practice 1) as you stand in front of the trash can.

11. Intentionally empty the contents of the dustpan into the trash can. Keep your eyes on the contents as they flow from the dustpan into the trash.

12. Intentionally put the dustpan down. Notice where you put it and the way you bend down toward the floor. Then, intentionally pick up the broom again.

13. Continue mindful sweeping until the timer goes off. Feel free to extend your practice if you haven't finished the task when the timer goes off, or to sweep another area if you finish before the timer goes off.

14. When you are done, intentionally place the broom back where you usually store it.

15. Take one diaphragmatic breath: inhale through the nose, and exhale through pursed lips.

16. Validate your practice.

Increasing Your Awareness

- See if you can describe in a few words what mindful sweeping was like. You can write this down if you like.

- Did you catch your mind wandering at all? If so, where did it go? Remember, this is not about judging what happened. It's about awareness.

- If your mind wandered, were you able to gently redirect your attention back to the sweeping task? Can you describe that experience as well?

18. Mindful Walking

Mindful walking allows for a greater awareness of your body and what it can do. It's more common to go from point A to point B in autopilot mode, oftentimes without thinking about how you've walked from one place to another. This practice will help you hone in on your present-moment experience, step by literal step, such that you are not on autopilot and can savor your experience. More conscious attention to your walking will also cultivate gratitude for your body.

In 2013, the journal *Evidence-Based Complementary and Alternative Medicine* published evidence from a randomized controlled trial investigating the effectiveness of a mindful walking program in patients with high levels of perceived psychological distress.[30] The study included participants between the ages eighteen and sixty-five who were moderately to highly distressed. They were randomly selected either for eight sessions of mindful walking over four weeks or for no intervention at all. Results indicated that patients in the mindful walking program showed reduced psychological distress symptoms and increased scores on quality-of-life scales compared with patients who received no intervention. With psychological and physiological benefits, mindful walking is a way to feel a greater connection to your breath and, literally, to the earth under your feet.

Note: If you are in a wheelchair, see if you can modify this practice so that you notice each time you engage with the wheels. If you are using a walker or a cane, you can modify this practice to suit your needs as well. The idea is to create a mindful awareness of each micromovement that gets you from one place to another.

Setup

- You can engage in this exercise any time you walk, such as on the way to your car or public transportation before or after work, on a lunch break, or even down your apartment building hallway.

- You can practice anywhere—for example, on the sidewalk, if it isn't too crowded, or in a park. However, I would caution you from doing it when there is a lot of foot traffic or when you need to cross a major intersection, since your safety needs to come first.

- You can walk barefoot, if it's safe to do so, or you can choose to wear comfortable shoes. Either way will offer benefits.

- Set a timer for five minutes.

Practice

1. Start by standing upright with your feet planted firmly on the ground.

2. Open your eyes and gaze forward in the direction you will be walking.

3. Take a moment to note the sensations at the bottom of your feet, from your toes to your heels.

4. Continue to feel rooted, and find your balance.

5. Next, very slowly and methodically, lift your right foot from the ground, and observe what that feels like.

6. Notice the weight shifting onto the left leg, and observe what that feels like.

7. Having peeled your right foot off the ground, move it forward ever so slightly and place it back down on the ground ahead of you. Observe what that feels like.

8. Notice as you balance on both feet again even though your right foot is now in front of the left.

9. Now begin to very slowly and methodically lift your left foot off the ground, and observe what that feels like.

10. Observe how the weight shifting onto the right leg feels.

11. Having peeled your left foot off the ground, observe as you move it forward ever so slightly and place it back on the ground ahead of you and your right foot.

12. Notice as you balance on both feet again, even though your left foot is now in front of the right.

13. If your mind wanders and you find it challenging to stay focused, redirect your attention—without judgment—back toward wherever you are in the practice. You can redirect as many times as you need.

14. Continue for five minutes, but feel free to extend your practice—or don't set a timer at all!

15. When you finish, stand still again and gaze forward. Inhale through your nose, hold for a moment, and then slowly and gently exhale through pursed lips.

16. At the end of the exhale, find your pause and, in the space of the pause, validate your practice.

Even when you aren't walking, you can use elements of this practice. For example, if you are at your desk and feel like grounding, pay attention to the sensation of your feet rooting to the ground. You can even pair walking mindfulness with an *inhale, hold, exhale, pause* sequence.

Increasing Your Awareness

- What did you notice as you engaged in this walking exercise? How did the experience of mindful walking differ from your usual experience of walking?

- What, if any, sensations did you notice in your whole body as you engaged in this exercise?

- Remind yourself that not every time you practice will you feel a certain way. If you felt bored, go with that. If you felt frustrated, go with that. The point of practice is to notice and observe, to slow down your movements and to recognize the mechanics that go into taking a single step.

- Notice how this exercise felt compared to other exercises, again, without judging one as "better" than the other.

19. Mindful Doodling

Many of us have been told not to doodle and, instead, to pay attention. As it turns out, doodling, or spontaneous drawing, helps us focus better and allows for more efficient recall of information. According to a rigorous study by psychologist Jackie Andrade, doodling is also helpful for memory retention.[31] There is also research linking doodling and art making to overall decreased psychological distress, suggesting that the rhythmic and repetitive action of mindful drawing or doodling actually reduces the levels of stress hormones, including cortisol, in the body.

In one study, forty adult participants spent forty-five minutes engaging in free-form art without any specific instruction.[32] Results indicated that nearly 75 percent of participants had lower cortisol levels afterward as measured from saliva samples taken before and after art making. No significant differences could be correlated to age, race, or prior artistic experience, speaking to the universality of the benefits of making art. Doodling also offers the space to express emotions in a more abstract way without fear or judgment. It also allows for creativity to flow. Sunni Brown writes and speaks about the act of doodling, arguing that it unlocks our brains and is a key component to learning.[33]

The irony is that many of us think of doodling as an absentminded and even unconscious activity, and yet it has so many benefits for the brain. By taking the opportunity to add more mindfulness to doodling, we also reap the benefits of mindfulness practice!

Setup

- Find a comfortable position conducive to drawing.

- Gather your drawing tools: colored pencils, crayons, markers, or chalk and a blank page. Or you can choose to draw on the sidewalk!

- Set a timer for five minutes.

Practice

1. Start by taking the chosen drawing tool in your hand, and hold it the way you would to draw.

2. Notice how it feels in your hand: the weight, the texture, how it feels against your fingers.

3. Begin by drawing a circle, but instead of just drawing it quickly, see if you can go slowly, savoring each movement.

4. Next draw a square, and again notice every movement necessary to make it: draw one line and then another, and then another, and then another. Notice as you draw how the object goes from one line to a two-sided creation, to three, and then four.

5. Do the same for a triangle.

6. Now, repeat steps 3 through 5 using a different part of the tool you're using. If you used the point of a pencil, now try with the edge of the sharpened pencil, for example.

7. Now choose a different color, if you'd like, and begin by doodling anything you want, without much forethought. Allow your hand to go in any which direction without picking it up from the page.

8. You can stay on one doodle until the timer goes off, or repeat step 7 as many times as you like for multiple doodles.

9. End the practice by putting your tool down.

10. Validate your practice.

Increasing Your Awareness

- Notice what it was like to move your hand across the page during each step.

- Without the urge to judge or compare, try to notice how it felt to draw each unique shape. If you notice no difference, that's noticing too.

- How did it feel to use the different sides of the drawing tool? Just notice. There is no right or wrong answer.

- How did the different colors (if you used multiple colors) add to the different parts of the drawing?

- Validate your shapes and doodles, no matter what they look like.

- Remind yourself that the exercise was about engaging in mindfulness practice and had nothing to do with skill or artistic output.

20. Mindful Coloring

As adults, we don't often leave time for coloring, or any type of creative play, for that matter. As it turns out, mindful coloring has a positive impact on well-being. DeLue's research found that coloring a mandala—a spiritual geometric design—helped reduce blood pressure, heart rate, and feelings of anxiety.[34] In another study using mandala coloring, Curry and Kasser also found postpractice decreases in anxiety.[35]

Nicola Holt designed two studies to measure the impact of coloring pictures.[36] In the first, forty-seven first-year undergraduates were asked to read and color for twenty minutes. Some were asked to read first; others were asked to color first. All of the participants reported feeling calmer, feeling more contented, and having more energy after coloring than they did after reading. Additionally, they reported a greater ability to attend to the present moment. In the second study, fifty-one undergraduates took part in the same reading and coloring activities. Researchers confirmed the results of the first study and, additionally, found that participants had improved visual attention and displayed more creative thinking.

This practice will help hone your ability to obtain these research-backed benefits. It also gives you permission to look away at times from the screens in your life and explore a more playful side of yourself.

Setup

- Find a comfortable position conducive to coloring.

- Gather your tools: colored pencils, crayons, markers, or chalk (whatever you fancy!) and a template of your choice. You can take one from a mindful coloring book or from an online source or use figure 2. You can also download this template at http://www. newharbinger.com/46080.

- Set a timer for five minutes.

Figure 2. Mandala

Practice

1. Start by taking the chosen coloring tool in your hand.

2. Notice how it feels: give attention to its weight and texture, and how it feels in your hand.

3. Hold it in your natural writing or drawing position and notice what that grip feels like.

4. Notice its color and see if the color elicits any feelings, sensations, or thoughts without judging them.

5. Notice what it looks like. Ask with curiosity. Is it smooth? Long? Pointy? Dull? What else do you notice?

6. Watch—as if you were an outside observer—as you bring your hand down to the page.

7. Begin to fill in a particular part of the template, and watch the color unfold on the page.

8. Notice the sound the coloring tool makes on the page.

9. Play with pressing down harder with your tool. Then try pressing down lightly. What changes about the color when you change pressure? What changes in your grip or in your breathing?

10. Play with using a different angle, such as going from point to side. What, if anything, do you notice?

11. For a moment, see if you can place your tool in your nondominant hand and maybe even try to color with it. What, if anything, do you notice about this experience? What sensations, thoughts, and feelings come up? Is it frustrating? Are you more focused? Just notice.

12. Feel free to change colors and repeat the previous steps, if you have time.

13. When the timer is up, see if you can stop where you are, even if you have not finished, and even if you were in the middle of a stroke.

14. Take one deep breath in through the nose, and exhale through pursed lips.

15. Validate yourself for completing your five minutes.

Increasing Your Awareness

- Validate yourself, as always, for showing up and taking time for yourself.

- See if you can bring mindful awareness to the completion of this experience by moving away from whether it was good or bad. Instead, notice if you felt relaxed while doing it or if you didn't feel a difference.

- With a sense of curiosity, observe what, if anything, came up for you when you attempted to color whichever template you chose.

Did you have an urge to color outside of the lines? Did coloring outside the lines irk you? Just notice without analyzing your feelings.

- Since you are unlikely to finish coloring in one sitting, notice if any thoughts, feelings, or body sensations came up about stopping. Just observe, with as much compassion as possible, and see if you can sit in that experience of not being able to finish.

21. Mindful Reading

It's said that a good book can change the course of our lives. Recent research suggests that the act of reading can actually extend our lives, too. Researchers out of Yale discovered that those who read live longer than those who don't. More specifically, those who read a book for over three and a half hours a week are likely to live twenty-three months longer than those who don't regardless of wealth, education, health, or gender. The researchers cited previous research and attributed what they called the "survival advantage" to two main factors. First, reading books fosters the "slow, immersive process" of "deep reading," a cognitive engagement that "occurs as the reader draws connections to other parts of the material, finds applications to the outside world, and asks questions about the content presented." Second, books "can promote empathy, social perception, and emotional intelligence, which are cognitive processes that can lead to greater survival."[37]

While it might be easy to get lost in an article or story, there are several ways to intentionally connect more deeply, not just with what you're reading and its applications, but with yourself, if you take a mindful approach. Reading has the innate capacity to take hold of the senses and place you firmly in the present moment. It's almost a fast track to mindfulness. This mindful reading practice will help plant you in the present and nourish your mind more fully.

Setup

- Find time when you can read more than a few paragraphs.

- Choose reading material that doesn't trigger a negative reaction.

- You may want to choose fiction or a book of poetry, or anything you feel most comfortable with. It can also be a magazine or newspaper article.

- If you want to read on a device, choose one that's specifically intended for reading.

- Set a timer for five minutes, or you can choose to engage in this practice for as long as you'd like.

Practice

1. Find a comfortable seated position.

2. Position the text so that you are not straining your eyes or your body.

3. Notice what the book or reading device feels like. Is it heavy? What's it like to hold it in your hands?

4. What does the cover look like? Notice the colors, the font of the title or subtitle.

5. Open the text and pay attention to the following (if reading from a book or a magazine or newspaper): How do the pages feel to touch? What do the pages smell like? Does the light in the room impact the text or create shadows on the page?

6. Take a diaphragmatic breath (see practice 1). Focus on the inhale and the exhale, allowing the exhale to be slightly longer than the inhale. Take a momentary pause.

7. Begin to read either out loud or in your head.

8. Consciously slow down your usual reading pace.

9. Notice the shape of each word on the page as you read it.

10. Notice the sound of each word as you read it. Do any stand out?

11. Do you notice a certain rhythm in your words?

12. Notice if certain words, sentences, or paragraphs elicit any type of response. Just take note without adding meaning to it.

13. If something distracts you from the words you're reading, simply recognize it. Maybe it's a bird chirping outside or a fire truck racing to a call. Once you note it, direct your attention back toward the text.

14. When you are ready, gently close the text.

15. Feel the weight of the reading material again. Think for a moment about how that book or newspaper or magazine article was created.

Can you imagine the author sitting at a desk writing what you just read? Can you picture a machine printing the text or imagine the smell of fresh ink?

16. Inhale through the nose and exhale through pursed lips.

17. Validate your practice and the time you took to complete it.

Increasing Your Awareness

- As you were reading, did thoughts about the practice come up, like *This feels strange* or *This is an interesting way to practice my mindfulness skills?* Just notice.

- Did you catch your mind wandering at all? If so, where did it go?

- Did any feelings or sensations distract you from practicing? If so, what did you notice?

- If your mind wandered, were you able to gently redirect your attention back to the text?

- Were you able to offer yourself compassion for needing to redirect your attention?

22. Mindful Bedtime

Just as you can wake up more mindfully, you can wind down mindfully for bed too. Many of us have difficulty falling asleep because our minds are overactive. Even though we are supposed to be winding down, we might lie in bed scrolling news headlines or thinking about our to-do list for the next day or for even two Sundays away. All of this creates stress.

Stress is often associated with insomnia, so being able to counteract it is imperative for sleep. One study confirmed that mindfulness practice is a sleep aid.[38] The study included a mindfulness group and a control group (sleep-education group). Results indicated that after six sessions, those in the mindfulness group experienced less insomnia, fatigue, and depression than the other group. The mechanisms behind why this works include mindfulness's ability to induce the relaxation response, which is the opposite of the stress-inducing fight-or-flight response. The relaxation response is associated with reduced blood pressure levels, a lower resting heart rate, and increased alpha brain waves. Alpha waves are a precursor to theta waves, which characterize the first stage of sleep.

A bedtime mindfulness practice allows you to open up with compassion to the frustrations and disappointments you have with events of the day. It also helps to create a calmer mind space, which is necessary to fall asleep and sleep efficiently.

Setup

- Start preparing for bed.

- Keep paper and a writing tool by your bed.

- Put on pajamas or whatever else you might wear to sleep.

- Don't use a timer for this one, because it might seem jolting. Instead, start this practice approximately five minutes before you are ready to go to bed (wash up and brush your teeth beforehand).

- If you'd like to, turn on a white noise machine that plays sounds from nature or whatever makes you feel calm.

Practice

1. Turn your devices off or turn on their sleep setting.

2. Charge your devices overnight in another room, or at the very least, don't keep them on your night table directly next to you.

3. Enter your bedroom and dim the lights.

4. Gently pull down the covers and get into bed.

5. Sit comfortably leaned up against a pillow.

6. Take three deep breaths in through the nose and out through pursed lips.

7. Take a minute or so to dwell on three highlights of your day (one could even be the mindful morning shower you took).

8. If thoughts intrude about what you didn't do or what you forgot to do today, see if you can notice those thoughts, without judgment, and remind yourself that the day is definitely over. All of that is in the past, and you no longer have control over what happened.

9. If it feels comfortable, let yourself know that you forgive yourself for anything you perceive to be undone or you think you could have handled better.

10. If your mind is turning like a hamster wheel, and no amount of breath work is helping, take this opportunity to spend no more than forty-five seconds writing down everything your mind is telling you. This way, it's now on paper and out of your mind.

11. Go from sitting to lying down, and notice how the transition feels.

12. Make a brief assessment of the weight of your body on the mattress, the weight of your head on the pillow.

13. Make a brief assessment of your temperature, and adjust accordingly (for example, add or remove a blanket).

14. Close your eyes.

15. Take five breaths in, focusing on the sensation of the inhale and the sensation of the exhale.

16. It's natural that your mind might continue to wander to events of the day or the day ahead. Continue to notice where your mind goes with compassion, and then redirect your attention back to the sensation of breathing in and breathing out.

17. If you are still awake after an hour, go into another room with dim lighting and practice mindful reading (see practice 21) for ten to fifteen minutes. Then return to bed and try this exercise again.

18. Ideally, you will fall asleep and stay asleep. Validate your practice the morning after!

Increasing Your Awareness

The next morning, refer to the postpractice awareness questions at the end of chapter 3. (Note: If you had trouble falling asleep, remember that this is a process.) Some nights you may be more efficient at this than others, and that's okay.

PART 4

Mindful Living

23. Radical Acceptance

The first step to mindful living is radically accepting the present moment for what it is. This doesn't mean rolling over and passively resigning to whatever circumstances you are experiencing. What it means is completely accepting that the reality of this moment is, in fact, the reality of this moment, and that resisting reality not only is impossible but also creates stress, suffering, and sometimes even learned helplessness.

"Radical acceptance" was first coined by Marsha Linehan while she was creating dialectical behavioral therapy (DBT), which was one of the early psychological interventions to incorporate mindfulness practice.[39] The term is based on the idea that although we can't control—for the most part—how life unfolds, we can control how we perceive or react to life unfolding. Fighting against reality, even if that reality is painful, is likely to cause suffering beyond that of the reality itself. Radical acceptance also has roots in Buddhism. One of the main tenets of Buddhism is the concept of nonattachment—since it is believed that attachment is the root of all suffering.

Through radical acceptance, you seek nonattachment to anything other than the present moment. When you attach to fantasies—what life should or would have been like or what life should or could be—in the present moment you continue to live either in the past, which you can't redo, or in a future you know nothing about yet. When you radically accept present-moment reality, you ground yourself firmly and with less judgment, anger, and denial into that reality. In this way, the goal of rooting into the present can actually help you grow and move forward rather than cling to fantasies and stagnate.

As a caveat: Radical acceptance is not, in any way, meant to condone a dangerous situation that requires you to make a change, such as taking action to leave an abusive relationship.

Practice

1. Think of a situation that is emotionally or physically uncomfortable for you.

2. Notice your resistance to the reality of the situation by asking yourself and mentally noting the answers to the following questions with as little judgment as possible: *Do I constantly wish that things were different? Do I often think that I'd be happier and more joyful if only this changed? Do I ruminate about past, less-painful times or future times when this will be over?*

3. Taking a cue from a DBT phrase, see if you can gently "turn your mind" toward acceptance. Since that's very abstract, imagine this scenario: You are stopped in your tracks by a fork in the road. One path goes toward acceptance of present-moment reality, and the other toward rejection of it. Can you imagine, even for a moment, how going down each path might make you feel? Can you feel the

increased suffering that might arise if you chose to walk down the path of rejection? Even if it doesn't take away the pain, can you feel an ounce calmer as you walk down the acceptance path?

4. Continue to visualize the path of acceptance.

5. Notice, without judgment, any thoughts, feelings, and sensations that come up.

6. Now, deliberately try to imagine you have accepted the uncomfortable situation. Remember, radical acceptance doesn't mean that you just lie down and resign passively to your life; it means you understand that you can't change the present moment, even if you want to, and that to resist it will feel worse.

7. If it feels comfortable to do so, place either hand over your heart center.

8. Notice how it feels to radically accept, even if you are just imagining it, without expectations of how it ought to feel.

9. Take a diaphragmatic inhale, and then exhale (see practice 1).

10. Say silently or out loud to yourself, "It's okay sweetheart, it's okay."

11. Repeat steps 9 and 10 as many times as you'd like.

You can repeat this practice with the same painful experience, as needed, to help you accept it, or you can repeat this practice with another experience. If you are triggered at any time, please stop the practice (and reach out to a mental health professional for support, if needed). If this practice works for you, try to devote at least a week to it, or you might consider extending it beyond a week or trying it for one week and then returning to it at a later time. If this practice is helpful, practice it routinely.

24. Self-Compassion

According to pioneering researcher Kristin Neff, *self-compassion* entails extending yourself the same goodwill and kindness that you would another person you care about during difficult times. Many clinicians favor cultivating self-compassion to building up self-esteem, as the former is geared toward accepting all of your imperfections with kindness. In some ways, self-compassion is like wrapping yourself in unconditional care and grace.[40]

This still means you are accountable for the way you show up for yourself and others. It doesn't mean you say to yourself, *The heck with trying to grow, because I unconditionally love myself anyway.* But it does mean that you don't have to beat yourself up, tear yourself down, or rage at yourself, mercilessly. It is possible to both offer yourself compassion and hold yourself accountable for any change you can make that is actually within your control. It is possible to afford yourself the utmost kindness as you discern what is and isn't within your control to change. It is important for your actual well-being to love yourself in spite of the fact that you are not and never will be perfect. Much research confirms the robust role of practicing self-compassion in buffering against the development and maintenance of psychological challenges, including depression and anxiety.[41]

Practice

1. Choose a situation or perceived inadequacy in your life that you are ashamed of, dislike, or are highly critical of, and write it down (for example, "I often avoid expressing my opinions at work").

2. Take some time to write in detail about this perceived inadequacy, including how it makes you feel, what kind of thoughts come up about it, and any examples of negative self-talk that arise in response to it. Just jot down the first things that come to mind.

3. Read what you wrote out loud to yourself and notice how it makes you feel.

4. Put that paper aside.

5. Think of someone you trust and who loves you unconditionally.

6. On a different sheet of paper, take a few moments to write a letter to yourself from that person who came to mind.

7. Address the letter with "Dear _____." Fill in the blank with your name. Then continue on the next line with what this person would say to you about your character and your alleged inadequacy. Try to be detailed, and instead of *you are not…* statements, focus on *you are…* statements that come from a place of respect and love. For example, "You are someone people respect, and your opinion at work would be valued in important meetings."

8. Place one hand over your heart and, holding the letter in the other hand, read it out loud to yourself and notice how it makes you feel.

9. Sit with the notion that although this letter was from someone you thought of, you actually wrote these words.

10. Reread the letter whenever you need.

You can repeat this practice with a different perceived inadequacy and a letter from the same person or another person who loves you. Try to devote at least a week to this practice. You might consider extending this practice beyond a week or trying it for a week and then returning to it at a later time.

25. Self-Love

To be loved and accepted is a basic human need. Now consider that you can offer that very need to yourself! Self-love includes showering yourself with warmth, forgiveness, gentleness, and an authentic desire to nurture yourself. The challenge is that most of us have an inner critic who tries to cast doubt, undermine achievements, and tell us we're not good enough. This critic attempts to put a mountain in front of our own attempts at self-love. It may even tell us that we're not worthy of receiving it.

There is a common misconception that to engage in self-love is to engage in a selfish endeavor. That is far from the truth, because the only way to even begin to show up for others in your life is to offer yourself love. The irony, too, is that upon engaging in self-love, you make healthier choices about who to allow into your life. Self-love is crucial for your well-being. A study out of the University of Exeter asked volunteers to listen to self-love-oriented audio clips. Results indicated that after eleven minutes, their heart rate decreased compared to that of those who were told to pay attention to their inner critic.[42]

So, what exactly is self-love? Self-love is a dynamic mind-set. It is more than simply the state of feeling good about yourself or singing your own praises. It is about respecting yourself and honoring all that you are, including your strengths and vulnerabilities. It's the process of getting in touch with what you are thinking and feeling, and instead of feeding the wrath of an inner critic standing by ready to shame you, you notice all you experience with gentleness and nonjudgment. When you are in a self-loving place, you don't attach yourself to outside sources to find validation or fill a void you might feel. Instead, you step into a stance of loving yourself and naturally moving toward your own physical, psychological, and spiritual growth.

Self-love grows proportionately to how you nurture and treat yourself. With that, there are strategies and practices that can help silence your inner critic. What follows are some practice approaches you can take to cultivate self-love. These don't need to be executed in a step-by-step fashion. Choose what resonates and build on it, if and when it feels right.

Practice

Morning mirror love. When you get up in the morning and head to the bathroom, look at yourself in the mirror and find three things that you like.

Challenge your inner critic. That self-critic can often get loud and boisterous. It can be really convincing, and often what it says feels very real. Remind yourself that what this inner critic says feels real, but it is not true. The inner critic weaves negative, unhelpful stories that don't serve your highest interests. It isn't easy, but it is possible to put your inner critic in its proper place. It will likely always be there, yet by noting it without judgment and by not believing it, the lower and more inaudible the voice will become.

Drop the comparison game. When you compare yourself to others, it's an apples and oranges situation, since there is no one exactly like you. Comparing yourself to others leads nowhere healthy. It is a losing battle each and every time. Instead, ask, *What is something unique I love about myself?*

Connect with self. Take more time for yourself. This can include the five-minutes-a-day commitment to practice mindfulness, more time to read, more quiet time to reflect, or more time to journal. Whatever it is, it is your time.

Nurture your body. Stay hydrated, eat food that gives you energy, take a nap if needed, stretch, and get some movement in.

Say good-bye to toxicity. Part of self-love is setting boundaries, and part of setting boundaries is not allowing toxic relationships into your mental space. Practice no longer tolerating anyone who makes you feel shame, negativity, or unworthy.

Say yes and no. Say yes more often to the experiences and people helping you connect to your most authentic self. On the flip side, avoid people pleasing, and say no to experiences and people when they are not helping you connect to your most authentic self, even if you think you have to say yes.

Embrace patience. Self-love is a process. See self-compassion (practice 24)!

Have a go-to mantra to tell yourself when you need a jolt of self-love. Choose one that resonates with you. Here are some examples: "I am more than enough." "I am loveable." "I will continue to show myself love and care." "Even though loving myself is a new experience, I am practicing each day."

Try to devote at least a week to this practice. You might consider extending it beyond a week or trying it for a week and then returning to it at a later time.

26. Mindful Listening

Mindful listening is a core element of healthy communication. Yet if you're like most people, you've had the experience of listening on auto-pilot: you think you are listening, only to realize as someone stops speaking that you have no idea what was said. Perhaps you were distracted by a notification on your device, a repetitive noise outside, or your mind wandering back to a news article you recently read. It's hard to shut out distractions completely, especially in this day and age when distractions abound.

Or, maybe you only half heard what was said, as the subject matter sent you into a fear-based place. It's a common reaction: when someone says something we don't like, instead of really listening and then thinking it through, we feel threatened, which activates the amygdala that readies us to attack back.

Really taking the time to listen to how another person feels—without immediately and sometimes impulsively reacting—creates the space for both parties to feel heard and then to show up with kindness and a more mindful ear. This can be done in any dyad, romantic or otherwise. In this way, you take a moment to pause and reflect on why you feel threatened and then proceed to truly listen without being on the defensive.

Mindfully listening, you might still come up against distractions and triggers, but you can practice noticing your distractibility and triggers without judgment and try to redirect your attention to the speaker and the words flowing from them. You can practice cultivating compassion for feeling the need to lash out; you can also work toward becoming more attuned to why you are feeling triggered and learn to take a pause before reacting.

While this might feel like a more formal practice because of its structure, I think of it as a mindful living practice because it is essentially a tool to strengthen the quality of your relationships.

Practice

1. Find a partner for this exercise.

2. Set a timer for two minutes.

3. One person begins to speak about whatever they would like, which can include how they feel about the relationship or about anything at all. It's good to keep the topics light, since this exercise is about practicing uninterrupted listening.

4. The listening partner practices listening. Nonverbal responses are okay, but verbal responses are not permitted at this time.

5. After two minutes, the listener takes a moment to quickly jot down one to three key points the speaker presented, as well as what, if

anything, they noticed triggering them or distracting them from listening.

6. Set the timer again for two minutes.

7. Now switch roles so that the initial speaker becomes the listener.

8. After two minutes, the listener takes a moment to quickly jot down one to three key points the speaker presented, as well as what, if anything, they noticed triggering them or distracting them from listening.

9. After each of you has spoken, notice together what thoughts, feelings, or body sensations were elicited during this experience. Notice together, with compassion and nonjudgment.

10. Thank one another for the time taken out of your busy schedules to strengthen your relationship.

Try to devote at least a week to this practice. You might consider extending this practice beyond a week or trying it for a week and then returning to it at a later time.

27. Mindful Media

Many of us consume media every day, throughout the day. The choices we make as to how and when we consume this media impacts our well-being. Too much time on the internet has been linked to an increased risk of depression.[43] Of course, the music, news, TV, and virtual connecting that is now at our fingertips is awesome in many ways. In theory, we have greater access to information, and information allows us a greater sense of perceived control.

Yet doesn't it seem all too easy today to dive into your favorite device instead of looking up and out and into the eyes of those around you? Isn't it too easy to be sucked down a rabbit hole of information that only serves to upset you? I'm talking about the repeated news cycle, the literal moment-by-moment updates of tragedies and disasters, and the medical advice you try to get from good old Dr. Google, which can send you into a hypochondriacal, catastrophic mind-set.

The answer isn't to eliminate all media, since in moderation you can benefit from your interactions online. It's to form a practice around media that allows you to be more consciously aware of how you are engaging so that you aren't left to our own autopilot devices!

Here are some general suggestions for how to bring more mindfulness to your consumption of media. You're bringing your senses to what you consume, so you know when to leave feeling fully informed.

Approach these suggestions like you might a buffet. Choose what resonates and leave the rest. Go at your own pace, in any order you'd like. These suggestions are designed for you to use at any time so that you can approach media with greater awareness of what you're consuming.

Practice

First off, always approach media with conscious intention:

- Don't reach for your phone first thing in the morning or right before you go to sleep.

- If you get a notification on your phone, before opening any application, take a diaphragmatic breath (see practice 1), and only then proceed.

- Notice your impulse to grab your phone when you are bored or anxious instead of sitting with these feelings. See if you can sit with these experiences for a little bit longer, or if you engage in any other mindfulness practice in this book.

- Become aware of your patterns. When do you most often use your phone? Note without judgment, and see if you can slowly make a change.

- Each time you take a step to consume media, consider setting an actual intention, such as *I am going to read this in order to learn something new or to have a greater understanding of this topic* or *I want to retain this information to tell someone I love later.*

- Consider setting a time intention. For example, *I am going to use social media or catch up on the news for thirty minutes total and then power down.*

Following these tips will bring more mindfulness to your daily use of media. Here are a few more ways to be mindful.

Consider the impact. Before scrolling through social media or online news, take a moment to consider the impact of whatever it is you are about to consume. You can ask yourself, *Do I have a sense that what I am about to engage with is going to inform me and possibly bring me joy or a feeling of connectivity? Or do I have a sense that what I am about to engage with is going to fuel my frustration, create anxiety, or make me jealous?* Follow your instincts based on your answers to these questions.

Choose what you consume. Take the time to consciously choose what you are consuming. This might mean becoming more aware of the violent slurs in the music you are listening to or the violence in a television series you usually watch before bed; even if the music or show is something you enjoy, it might be releasing stress hormones and disturbing your sleep. Also, don't be afraid to clear your social media feeds of anyone or anything that feels toxic to your well-being. Watch out especially for those profiles that make you feel less than or that elicit shame or trigger a comparison that is not healthy.

Check in with yourself. Make a point to check in with yourself while consuming media. This means that any time you consume a piece of media, pay attention to any response arising from your mind and body, without judgment. Watch for a stress response or feelings of anxiety, and let what you learn guide the rest of your consumption. Also, if you are reading a news story on your computer or phone, make a point to pause after every few paragraphs to take a diaphragmatic breath.

Increase your conscious awareness. Are you consciously aware of each moment as it unfolds? Check in with yourself if you start to lose track of the present moment. When something becomes a blur, start to focus on each TV character as they speak or the lyrics of the music you are listening to, or keep an eye on the colors on your screen or the way you use your finger to scroll down or switch applications.

Exercise nonjudgment and validation. Validate each and every step you take toward practicing mindful media. Validation can include telling yourself *I did a great job* or *I'm trying, and every time is another opportunity to approach it with more mindfulness.* No matter what, see if you can extend less judgment toward yourself as feelings arise. Also try to extend this nonjudgment to others. If you see a feed that doesn't sit well with you, see if you can also extend nonjudgment to the person behind a given post.

Try to devote at least a week to practicing some of these ways to be more aware of the media you consume. You might consider extending this practice beyond a week or trying it for a week and then returning to it at a later time.

28. Gratitude

Many suggest that having an attitude of gratitude is the key to a more mindful life. The research concurs: cultivating gratitude has been linked to decreased anxiety and depression and to overall greater well-being.[44] In fact, gratitude has become a self-help buzzword. It turns out that the benefits of saying thank-you aren't just grand delusions or a bunch of fluff.

According to Robert Emmons, a renowned gratitude expert, gratitude has two parts. First, "it's an affirmation of goodness. We affirm that there are good things in the world, gifts and benefits we've received." Then, "we recognize that the sources of this goodness are outside of ourselves."[45] This definition allows gratitude to become a way for you to hone in on what you have instead of always reaching for something new in the hope that it will make you happier. You can feel satisfied even if your every physical and material need is not met. Gratitude also allows you to trust in something greater than yourself, and let go of trying to control every detail of your life, which can be anxiety provoking.

Emmons and McCullough conducted a series of three studies in which they compared the well-being of those who kept a daily gratitude list with those who kept either a neutral list or a negative list.[46] Of note, none of the participants started the study more grateful than any of the others, nor did they change their life circumstance during the course of the study so that they'd have more to be grateful for. Results across the studies indicated that the participants who focused on gratitude had a more positive and optimistic appraisal of their life, greater positive mood, decreased negative mood, greater sleep quality, and a sense of connectedness with others.

Here is a practice that will help you cultivate gratitude in your own life.

Practice

1. Set a timer for five minutes.

2. During these five minutes, write a list of anything you feel gratitude for or want to express thanks for.

3. If you are stuck, you can write the same thing over and over again until the buzzer is up. This practice is all about showing up and taking the time to literally write your thanks.

4. If you struggle to find something you are grateful for in any given moment, then write that you are grateful for taking the time to express thanks even though you are not sure what you are thankful for.

5. Feel free to be specific, such as "I am thankful for the hot water during my shower this morning," or more general, such as "I am grateful for this day."

See if you can devote at least a week to this practice. You might consider extending this practice beyond a week or trying it for only one week and then returning to it at a later time.

29. Appreciation

How many times do you say thank you to a clerk or at the end of an email because it's a routine, habit, or social norms? It's not that you're not appreciative; it's just that your brain falls into certain patterns of working, and you don't necessarily notice the details of your experience. The human brain is wired to work fast and well, but to do things quickly, it uses familiar thinking pathways. Appreciation helps you slow down the thinking process long enough to notice what's around you so that you are no longer on autopilot mode. In other words, when you appreciate, you are truly paying attention on purpose and in the present moment to whom or what you appreciate.

Appreciation is also about deepening the connection you feel for what you are grateful for (see practice 28) by being more mindful. You can be grateful for things or people in your life without really appreciating them, but it's difficult to appreciate them and not be grateful. That's where mindfulness comes into play.

Mindfulness helps bridge the gap between gratitude and appreciation. When you are paying attention to the present moment, with authentic purpose, you can internalize and savor the true value and significance of your experience. The following mindfulness writing practice will assist you in expressing appreciation.

Practice

1. Set a timer for five minutes.

2. Identify an item, person, or concept you rarely notice and write it down. It can be how certain bodily functions work so seamlessly; it can be a person, like the security guard where you work; or it can be the process by which your food got to your table. There are many possibilities.

3. Ask yourself the following about what you've written down: *What is the first thing I notice about this? What impact does this have on my life? To what extent would my life be different without this? What does it take for this process to work as it does? And if I don't know, can I spend a few moments learning more about it to gain a greater sense of appreciation?* Write down your answers.

4. Read all that you've written and reflect on what thoughts and feelings come up for you, without judgment.

5. If you feel inclined, share what you've written with someone you care about.

6. Each day, try to find something different to appreciate, and be gentle with yourself if it takes time to find something.

Repeat this practice for at least a week, and then feel free to continue longer if you'd like. Or give it a try for just one week and circle back to it at another time down the road.

30. Beyond the Sixth Minute

I want to thank you for taking this journey with me. I also want to remind you—and myself—that mindfulness practice doesn't end here. It never does! I like to say, practice makes practice. While greater well-being is completely attainable, as humans we are truly always practicing.

As you lean into your mindfulness journey, there is no such thing as getting better. There is *going deeper*, however, meaning establishing a deepening intimacy with your own intrinsic ability to pay attention on purpose, in the present moment, and without judgment, even when life is challenging. Mindfulness practice can provide you with *quick calm*, if you are open to it. Practice itself is a call to action that moves you toward a lifelong relationship with mindfulness.

I'm going to end with five important reminders to help you make mindfulness a lifelong journey, even when you may not feel motivated to practice.

1. Make it a habit. Continue to make mindfulness practice a part of your daily routine, and commit to tacking it on to anything you regularly do, like brushing your teeth, or to a specific time of day, every day. Toothbrushing can be a mindful endeavor in and of itself (practice 12).

2. Consistency is key. Five minutes a day every day is more effective than one hour a week, and promotes a more continuous practice.

3. Start over. There are no endings to the beginnings you can take. Start over in any practice as much as you need to.

4. Be gentle with yourself. There's no becoming an expert. There's just practice.

5. Validate what you're doing. Validate your practice always (*I am worthy of taking these five minutes for myself each day*).

I hope you've felt me with you during your practices, and I want to commit to being here with you as you nurture yourself going forward. Remember, gentleness is the bridge between you and your mindfulness practice. Stay gentle, gentle, gentle with yourself, here, now, and beyond.

Afterword

People always ask me how I manage to meditate each day without missing a beat. They ask how I find time to journal and then share my thoughts on my blog or social media platforms. My response to them is simply this: How do you manage to brush your teeth each morning? How do you remember to put clothes on each morning before you leave the house? Why do you walk your dog several times a day?

The bottom-line answer is simple: It's a habit.

When Dr. Wolkin asked me to write her afterword, I enthusiastically accepted and anxiously awaited the manuscript of this exquisite book--which you've now had the fortune of reading as well. As I read through this roadmap and extrapolated its many gifts, the one resounding word that kept coming up for me over and over again was the word "habit."

Because what's more important than our habits?

Nothing.

Through a study published by Duke University, we know that habits–"good" or "bad"—form about 45 percent of our total behaviors. And our habits are behaviors that we frequently repeat, compounding their significance in the makeup of our lives. Habits are our foundation, and when one's foundation is weak, things start to crumble.

As a mindfulness teacher working with many different segments of the population across the world, I can attest that people who fail at making changes in their lives are those who fail to instill new habits. And those who are unsuccessful at instilling new habits often find themselves failing because they try to take on too much at once. Simply put: if a new habit requires more willpower than a person has at the moment they commit to it, they will fail—and the inverse is true as well.

My grandfather used to use a phrase that I always thought was strange when I was a child but later understood when I grew older and wiser. "You can't eat an elephant whole," he would pronounce. "But, you can eat it one bite at a time." Of course, as a child, I would literally think about the horror of eating an elephant! But later I learned that this proverbial elephant is the one that sits on our chest most of our lives and holds us back from living the best, freest version of ourselves. This elephant is any obstacle we face in our lives. Very rarely can we overcome such an obstacle with one swift change; instead, it requires steady, incremental changes in the form of habits—one small bite at a time.

This incremental journey, with Dr. Wolkin as our guide, allows us to build, one week at a time, the habits we need to cultivate in order to live our best lives. This is a book you can—and should—return to again and again like a mindful companion, helping create that strong foundation that all else can be built soundly upon. Easily done? Unlikely. Without inconsistencies? Absolutely not. We travel slowly and steadily, understanding that those who are inconsistent or quit the journey are often not lazy people. Instead, they are more often than not people who try their best but move too quickly and ambitiously.

The development of habits fails when we focus on pushing towards glory. But the development of habits that stick doesn't just require that short burst of motivation and willpower. (Motivation naturally drops after we get started with the quest, and just living our daily life can deplete willpower.) Furthermore, the habitual, unconscious part of our brain just does not respond well to the glory-seeking of a hero's journey—big sudden changes turn on our fight-or-flight response, which is unsustainable.

And, as Dr. Wolkin knows well, while we may think that just five minutes of practice a day is unimpressive to our executive brain (the part that loves big, lofty changes!), it is just what our unconscious brain needs (and it avoids waking up the amygdala, so to speak). Consistency creates incremental changes that lead us to the long-term goal of mental health and stability, building tools that we can rely on when the going gets tough.

May the going never get tough for you. But if it does, may you have the knowing that, having worked through this book, you now possess the tools and knowledge to experience the waves with ease, free from suffering.

—Shelly Tygielski

Acknowledgments

I might be biased, but I won the parent lottery. Thank you, Mom, for your courage, passion, joie de vivre, and overall brilliance and know-how. Thank you, Dad, for your genuine kindness, generosity of spirit, sensitivity, and sense of humor. You are my forever teachers.

To my siblings, Erin and Josh Gelfand, there are no words for the way you welcome me into your home, which is my writing retreat. Without your boundless love and generosity, I would not have been able to put this out into the world.

Thank you to my Gelfand-Christie siblings and exquisite extended family of aunts, uncles, and cousins here and around the world: all of you constantly inspire me in your own unique ways. Fortunate to share a gene pool with you.

To my dearest draft readers and mentor-friends: I give a thousand thanks to author Kim Constantinesco. Your commitment to helping me see this vision through has touched me beyond words. You are my model for mindful living with grace and kindness. A *sheynem dank* to you and Shasta the Wonder Dog. Soul Camp Creative cofounder Ali Leipzig, thank you for your thoughtful read-through and support. Dr. Jessica Delman, *gracias por todo*. You helped me get this off the ground and running. Olympic and world champ Tianna Bartoletta for consistently letting me know "you are elite at always doing the very best you can in any single moment." Your cheerleading was endless and took me past the finish line. I couldn't imagine anyone else writing the foreword to this book. Julie Sahlein, Alison Lyons, Mary Wetherill, Dr. Afton Bergel, and Sydney Faith Rose for the constant support in each of your special ways. You truly witnessed and guided this journey, and I love you all so much. Dr. Kristel Carrington for your brilliant collaboration, and for allowing me to teach and learn in the very same instant. Sheena Levi, for the brainstorming from the inception of my private practice, blog, and beyond. Dr. Stanley A. Gelfand, your passion for science and textbook writing has inspired my own writing. Shelly Tygielski, *todah rabah*, friend. Your words add much meaning to this work.

Dr. Rebecca E. Wells, choosing me as the neuropsychologist for a mindfulness-based stress reduction and mild cognitive impairment study literally changed the course of my life. Your passion for the brain and its endless potential for healing continues to inform my work.

My extended Harvard family, including fellow postdoc and gem of a friend Dr. Laura K. Phillips; mentor in life and neuropsych, the incomparable Dr. John Miner; teachers Dr. Margaret O'Connor and Dr. Bill Stone. So many of the seeds for this project were planted a decade ago. Thank you for showing me the soil and how to water it (and practice patience).

It turns out the cliché is true: it takes a village! My village, all of you, had a part in this book coming to life: Jennifer Pastiloff, Maggie Smith, Eric Knoll, Jen Seltzer, Heather Jill, Angelika Zhu, Dr. Jason Siefferman, Dr. Jaime Zuckerman, Dr. Adrienne Meier, Chaya Cooper, Margaret Morton, Dr. Elizabeth Scott, Jennifer Mann, Joel Knopf, Emma Bolden, Enzo Silon Surin, Carrie Keskinen, Dr. Meredith

Bergman, Barbara Williams, Dr. Jessica Lewis, Michelle Garside, Laura Michaels, Baylee Decastro, Johnny Ray Falla, Dr. Eli Diamond, and Dr. Adena Steinberg.

There is almost nothing comparable in this world to the love and support of old friends who have witnessed elementary and middle-school dreams come true: infinite love for you all.

My IFS creative crew: what a beautiful surprise in my life during these challenging, unprecedented COVID-19 times. Adrienne Glasser, you're a gifted teacher.

My Queens College MFA crew: you inspire me with your words and advocacy toward making this place a more mindful place to live. Thank you, adepts Nicole Cooley and Kimiko Hahn, Dr. Jason Tougaw and Dr. Briallen Hopper, John Rice, Lucy Torres, Krista Crommett, Kara Pernicano, Deborah Fried-Rubin, Julia Tolo, Catherine LaSota, and all my professors and classmates.

My past, present, and future clients: endless gratitude for allowing me to bear witness to and humbly collaborate with you on your journey toward greater well-being.

To my Instagram community: I am overwhelmed by your support and our shared passion for ending mental health stigma! Humbled by your thought-provoking comments, shares, and outpouring of enthusiasm for this book. Gentle, Gentle, Gentle, XO, Dr. Jen.

Brady Kahn, you nailed this book's copyediting. I couldn't have asked for more on-point work.

Finally, to my editor, Ryan Buresh: this book became what it is because of your generous guidance. My deepest gratitude.

Endnotes

1   Nyanaponika Thera, *The Heart of Buddhist Meditation: A Handbook of Mental Training on the Buddha's Way of Mindfulness* (London: Rider, 1962).

2   Jon Kabat-Zinn, *Full Catastrophe Living* (New York: Dell Publishing, 1991).

3   Susan Nolen-Hoeksema, "The Role of Rumination in Depressive Disorders and Mixed Anxiety/Depressive Symptoms," *Journal of Abnormal Psychology* 109, no. 3 (2000): 504–11.

4   Tammi Kral et al., "Impact of Short- and Long-Term Mindfulness Meditation Training on Amygdala Reactivity to Emotional Stimuli," *NeuroImage* 181 (2018): 301–13.

5   Ronald Glaser et al., "Chronic Stress Modulates the Immune Response to a Pneumococcal Pneumonia Vaccine," *Psychosomatic Medicine* 62, no. 6 (2000): 804–7.

6   Michael S. Chin and Stefanos N. Kales, "Understanding Mind-Body Disciplines: A Pilot Study of Paced Breathing and Dynamic Muscle Contraction on Autonomic Nervous System Reactivity," *Stress Health* 35, no. 4 (2019): 542–48.

7   Britta K. Hölzel et al., "Mindfulness Practice Leads to Increases in Regional Brain Gray Matter Density," *Psychiatry Research* 191, no. 1 (2011): 36–43; William R. Marchand, "Neural Mechanisms of Mindfulness and Meditation: Evidence from Neuroimaging Studies," *World Journal of Radiology* 6, no. 7 (2014): 471–79.

8   Julie Corliss, "Mindfulness Meditation May Ease Anxiety, Mental
     Stress," *Harvard Health Blog*, January 9, 2014. https://www.health
     .harvard.edu/blog/mindfulness-meditation-may-ease-anxiety
     -mental-stress-201401086967.

9   Elizabeth A. Hoge et al., "Randomized Controlled Trial of Mindfulness
     Meditation for Generalized Anxiety Disorder:
     Effects on Anxiety and Stress Reactivity," *Journal of Clinical Psychiatry*
     74, no. 8 (2013): 786–92.

10   Britta K. Hölzel et al., "Neural Mechanisms of Symptom Improvements
     in Generalized Anxiety Disorder Following Mindfulness Training,"
     NeuroImage: Clinical 2 (2013): 448–58.

11   Jon Kabat-Zinn, Leslie Lipworth, and Robert Burney, "The Clinical Use
     of Mindfulness Meditation for the Self-Regulation
     of Chronic Pain," *Journal of Behavioral Medicine* 8, no. 2 (1985): 163–90.

12   David S. Black and George M. Slavich, "Mindfulness Meditation and
     the Immune System: A Systematic Review of Randomized Controlled
     Trials," *Annals of the New York Academy of Sciences* 1373, no. 1 (2016):
     13–24.

13   Richard J. Davidson et al., "Alterations in Brain and Immune Function
     Produced by Mindfulness Meditation," *Psychosomatic Medicine* 65, no. 4
     (2003): 564–70.

14   Anthony P. King et al., "Altered Default Mode Network (DMN) Resting
     State Functional Connectivity Following a Mindfulness-Based Exposure
     Therapy for Posttraumatic Stress Disorder (PTSD) in Combat Veterans
     of Afghanistan and Iraq,"
     Depression and Anxiety 33, no. 4 (2016): 289–99.

15   Charles Duhigg, *The Power of Habit: Why We Do What We Do
     in Life and Business* (New York: Random House, 2012).

16 Barbara L. Fredrickson et al., "Do Contemplative Moments Matter? Effects of Informal Meditation on Emotions and Perceived Social Integration," *Mindfulness* 10, no. 9 (2019): 1915–25.

17 Karin Chellew et al., "The Effect of Progressive Muscle Relaxation on Daily Cortisol Secretion," *Stress* 18, no. 5 (2015): 538–44.

18 Wolfgang Luthe and Johannes H. Shultz, *Applications in Psychotherapy: Autogenic Therapy*, vol. 3, ed. Wolfgang Luthe (New York: Grune and Stratton, 1969).

19 Friedhelm Stetter and Sirko Kupper, "Autogenic Training: A Meta-Analysis of Clinical Outcome Studies," *Applied Psychophysiology and Biofeedback* 27, no. 1 (2002): 45–98.

20 Joe Utay and Megan Miller, "Guided Imagery as an Effective Therapeutic Technique: A Brief Review of Its History and Efficacy Research," *Journal of Instructional Psychology* 33, no. 1 (2006): 40–43.

21 Marc J. Weigensberg et al., "Acute Effects of Stress-Reduction Interactive Guided Imagery on Salivary Cortisol in Overweight Latino Adolescents," *Journal of Alternative and Complementary Medicine* 15, no. 3 (2009): 297–303.

22 Jai Dudeja, "Benefits of Tadasana, Zhan Zhuang, and Other Standing Meditation Techniques," *International Journal of Research and Analytical Reviews* 6, no. 2 (2019): 607–18.

23 Johannes Graser and Ulrich Stangier, "Compassion and Loving-Kindness Meditation: An Overview and Prospects for the Application in Clinical Samples," *Harvard Review of Psychiatry* 26, no. 4 (2018): 201–15.

24 Stefan G. Hofmann, Paul Grossman, and Devon E. Hinton, "Loving-Kindness and Compassion Meditation: Potential for Psychological Interventions," *Clinical Psychology Review* 31, no. 7 (2011): 1126–32.

25 Jennifer S. Mascaro et al., "The Neural Mediators of Kindness-Based Meditation: A Theoretical Model," *Frontiers in Psychology* 6 (2015): 109.

26 Joseph B. Nelson, "Mindful Eating: The Art of Presence While You Eat," *Diabetes Spectrum: A Publication of the American Diabetes Association* 30, no. 3 (2017): 171–74.

27 Zaynah Khan and Zainab F. Zadeh, "Mindful Eating and Its Relationship with Mental Well-Being," *Procedia: Social and Behavioral Sciences* 159 (2014): 69–73.

28 Thich Nhat Hanh, *The Miracle of Mindfulness: An Introduction to the Practice of Meditation* (Boston: Beacon Press, 1999).

29 Adam W. Hanley et al., "Washing Dishes to Wash Dishes: Brief Introduction in an Informal Mindfulness Practice, Mindfulness 6 (2015): 1095–1103.

30 Michael Teut et al., "Mindful Walking in Psychologically Distressed Individuals: A Randomized Controlled Trial," *Evidence-Based Complementary and Alternative Medicine* 2013 (July 2013): Article ID 489856.

31 Jackie Andrade, "What Does Doodling Do?" *Applied Cognitive Psychology* 24, no. 1 (2010): 100–106.

32 Girija Kaimal, Kendra Ray, and Juan Muniz, "Reduction of Cortisol Levels and Participants' Responses Following Art Making," *Art Therapy* 33, no. 2 (2016): 74–80.

33 Sunni Brown, *The Doodle Revolution: Unlock the Power to Think Differently*, rep. ed. (New York: Portfolio, 2015).

34 Carol H. DeLue, "Physiological Effects of Creating Mandalas," in *Medical Art Therapy with Children*, ed. Cathy Malchiodi (London: Jessica Kingsley Publishers Ltd., 1999).

35 Nancy A. Curry and Tim Kasser, "Can Coloring Mandalas Reduce Anxiety?" *Art Therapy* 22, no. 2 (2005): 81–85.

36 Nicola J. Holt, Leah Furbert, and Emily Sweetingham, "Cognitive and Affective Benefits of Coloring: Two Randomized Controlled Crossover Studies," *Art Therapy* 36, no. 4 (2019): 200–208.

37 Avni Bavishi, Martin D. Slade, and Becca R. Levy, "A Chapter a Day: Association of Book Reading with Longevity," *Social Science and Medicine* 164 (2016): 44–48.

38 David S. Black et al., "Mindfulness Meditation and Improvement in Sleep Quality and Daytime Impairment Among Older Adults with Sleep Disturbances: A Randomized Clinical Trial," *JAMA Internal Medicine* 175, no. 4 (2015): 494–501.

39 Clive J. Robins, Henry Schmidt III, and Marsha M. Linehan, "Dialectical Behavior Therapy: Synthesizing Radical Acceptance with Skillful Means," in *Mindfulness and Acceptance: Expanding the Cognitive-Behavioral Tradition*, ed. Steven C. Hayes, Victoria M. Follette, and Marsha M. Linehan (New York: Guilford Press, 2004).

40 Kristin D. Neff, "The Role of Self-Compassion in Development: A Healthier Way to Relate to Oneself," *Human Development* 52, no. 4 (2009): 211–14.

41 Angus MacBeth and Andrew Gumley, "Exploring Compassion: A Meta-Analysis of the Association Between Self-Compassion and Psychopathology," *Clinical Psychology Review* 32, no. 6 (June 2012): 545–52.

42 Hans Kirschner et al., "Soothing Your Heart and Feeling Connected: A New Experimental Paradigm to Study the Benefits of Self-Compassion," *Clinical Psychological Science* 7, no. 3 (2019): 545–65.

43 Ariel Shensa et al., "Social Media Use and Depression and Anxiety Symptoms: A Cluster Analysis," *American Journal of Health Behavior* 42, no. 2 (2018): 116–28.

44 Kiralee Schache et al., "Gratitude—More Than Just a Platitude? The Science Behind Gratitude and Health," *British Journal of Health Psychology* 24, no. 1 (2019): 1–9.

45 Robert A. Emmons, "The Psychology of Gratitude: An Introduction," in *The Psychology of Gratitude*, ed. Robert A. Emmons and Michael E. McCullough (New York: Oxford University Press, 2004).

46 Robert A. Emmons and Michael E. McCullough, "Counted Blessings Versus Burdens: An Experimental Investigation of Gratitude and Subjective Well-Being in Daily Life," Journal of Personal and Social Psychology 84, no. 2 (2003): 377–89.

Jennifer R. Wolkin, PhD, is a licensed clinical health and neuropsychologist, writer, speaker, and mental health advocate. She founded a private practice with an appreciation that our mind, body, spirit, and brain are intimately intertwined and impacted by one another. She draws heavily on tools such as cognitive behavioral therapy (CBT) and mindfulness-based techniques. She is currently pursuing her master's degree in creative writing with a poetry focus. You can find her on Instagram @drjenpsych_.

MORE BOOKS from
NEW HARBINGER PUBLICATIONS

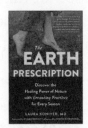

Did you know there are free tools you can download for this book?

Free tools are things like **worksheets, guided meditation exercises**, and **more** that will help you get the most out of your book.

You can download free tools for this book—whether you bought or borrowed it, in any format, from any source—from the **New Harbinger** website. All you need is a NewHarbinger.com account. Just use the URL provided in this book to view the free tools that are available for it. Then, click on the "download" button for the free tool you want, and follow the prompts that appear to log in to your NewHarbinger.com account and download the material.

You can also save the free tools for this book to your **Free Tools Library** so you can access them again anytime, just by logging in to your account! Just look for this button on the book's free tools page:

+ save this to my
free tools library

If you need help accessing or downloading free tools, visit **newharbinger.com/faq** or contact us at customerservice@newharbinger.com.

CELEBRATING
40 YEARS